Effective
e-Strategies

The Themes and Strategies at Work on the Web

HARRY R. TENNANT

Published by Stansbury Press
8423 Vista View Drive, Dallas, TX 75243 USA
http://www.stansburypress.com

ISBN: 0-9701500-0-8
Library of Congress Card Number: 00-104361

Publisher's Cataloging-in-Publication

Tennant, Harry.
    Effective e-strategies : the themes and strategies at work
on the web / Harry R. Tennant.
  —1st ed.
    p. cm.
    Includes bibliographical references and index.

    1. Electronic commerce. 2. Business planning
I. Title.
HF5548.32.T46 2000   658.8'4'0285
             QBI00-488

For Dianne...

With all my love and thanks for all the help

Contents

About the Author

Dr. Tennant formed Harry Tennant & Associates in 1993, focused on helping organizations build their Internet strategies, then implement them. They offer consulting and seminars on the new electronic commerce and marketing technologies that are changing the way companies do business. They build Web sites for clients, particularly those requiring technical sophistication. Customers include such well-known companies as Texas Instruments, Oracle, Southern Methodist University, MCI, Boy Scouts of America and Southern Comfort.

Prior to forming Harry Tennant & Associates, Dr. Tennant spent 14 years at Texas Instruments, was a TI Fellow, Chief Technologist of the Information Technology Group and conducted research into various aspects of computing technologies. He hosted and was responsible for the technical content of TI's series of internationally broadcast Artificial Intelligence Satellite Symposia.

Dr. Tennant is the author of the book, *Natural Language Processing: An Introduction to an Emerging Technology*, which appeared in 1981. He has published professional papers on natural language processing and computing environments as well as many popular articles on artificial intelligence and the future of computing.

Dr. Tennant was selected as one of 100 Outstanding Scientists under age 40 by *Science Digest* magazine. He earned his Ph.D. in Computer Science from the University of Illinois in 1980.

1 Introduction

The general who wins a battle makes many calculations before the battle is fought. The general who loses a battle makes but few calculations beforehand. Thus do many calculations lead to victory and few calculations to defeat; how much more no calculation at all!

— Sun Tzu, *The Art of War*

Strategy

An organization's *strategy* is its collection of top-level goals and its means for achieving them.

In this book, we will consider outward-looking strategies: not strategies concerned with the inner operations of businesses, but strategies that address

- serving customers,

- coordinating with suppliers and

- dealing with competition.

Serving customers

Businesses are human endeavors so they are as varied and unique as the people who run them and the people who buy from them. There are, however, common characteristics of the business-customer relationship, which will help organize our discussion of strategies.

Be known. Precisely. Potential customers must know the business before any money can change hands. The more precisely customers understand what a company offers the more likely they are to consider using their products. This may seem obvious, but many companies with attractive offerings fail for exactly this reason. And companies on the Net are particularly vulnerable. With hundreds of millions of Web pages out there, one of the biggest challenges for a new store is to come to mind when a consumer is ready to buy. It is not a simple thing to reserve a spot for your company and your products in the minds of each of your potential customers, but this is exactly what you must do.

Be the choice. No matter what a company offers, customers always have a choice. Typically, they can choose among similar offerings from many companies. In the case of commodities, customers can choose where to buy undifferentiated items from many vendors. And if there is no other choice, customers always have the option to choose to do nothing. Some of the more common issues of choice are:

- Solve a problem – Does the product or service do a better job of solving customers' problems than the competition?

- Easy and quick – Will the solution be easy to implement compared to its benefits?

- Value – Does the product or service provide good value for the customer?

- Comfort and trust – Is the customer comfortable doing business with the company?

Coordinating with suppliers

Network technology is changing the ways companies work with their suppliers. The amount of information about products and their parts is increasing. The information is becoming available more quickly, often in real time. Also the falling cost of transactions between a company and its suppliers is allowing seamless integration between companies and their suppliers.

The changing economics of transactions seem to be creating two quite different approaches to dealing with customers. The first is to use the opportunities for sharing information created by networks to build closer partnerships between companies and their suppliers. This approach focuses on sharing a lot more information about quality, demand, customer expectations and coordinated design. Information is routinely shared today which, in the past, would have been considered proprietary and hidden from suppliers. Companies were more concerned with leverage over suppliers than with cooperation.

The other approach to using the new economics of transactions for dealing with suppliers is to decrease the integration between a company and its suppliers. Cheap online transactions coupled with global reach has enabled auction—competitive bids for nearly every transaction. The advantage of dealing with suppliers through an auction is that it pressures the suppliers to reduce their costs so they can compete more effectively against the other bidders. The disadvantage is that it discourages tight coordination between companies and their key suppliers.

Which is the best way to take advantage of the lower transaction cost opportunity that networking has provided? It depends on your goals. If your goal is to force suppliers to reduce their costs, then the pressure of competitive bids is the right approach. It's their responsibility to figure out how to reduce costs. However, the goal could be more global cost reductions. For example, the automotive industry has about $200 billion in inventory, including finished automobiles awaiting sale and parts awaiting assembly. Imagine that the automotive industry could switch to a model where cars are built to order. That would eliminate the finished goods inventory. Then if an order for a car was instantly communicated through the car maker back to its suppliers for the parts specifically needed for that car, the parts could be delivered just as they are needed, not in bulk. In the ideal case, that eliminates parts inventory. $200 billion is freed, which is roughly 1.5 times the size of annual automobile sales of either General Motors or Ford. Incidentally, in addition to the cost savings, customers get exactly what they want, not what happens to be available on the lot. Impossible? It's already happening in the computer business.

How should the new economics of the Net be applied to working with suppliers?

- Know where you add value. Focus the efforts of your company where they will do the most good, where they will create the greatest value. Outsource the rest.

- Partner with the best. Partner with suppliers who are willing to work with you to reduce overall production costs while increasing customer value.

- Share clear expectations and help suppliers be successful. Provide suppliers with the information they need to help create products that better serve end customers. Interpret customer needs and understand suppliers' emerging technologies to create better products. Work closely with suppliers to improve quality, design, inventory, logistics and service, as well as reducing cost.

- Simplify. If there is a choice between close relationships with a few suppliers or distant relationships with many suppliers, opt for tighter integration.

- Focus on time. The critical element of mass markets was cost. As we move to mass customization of products, the critical element becomes time. The issue of $200 billion in inventory is an issue of time: As parts and vehicles get closer to being delivered as needed, as time delays are taken out of the supply chain, inventory costs approach zero.

Dealing with competition

Other companies have customer goals that are similar to yours. They want to reserve a presence in the mind of customers. They want to be the customer's choice, the solution to his problem that is quick and easy, a good value and the one the customer would feel comfortable dealing with. In fact, they want to be *first* in the customer's mind, the *best* solution, the *easiest* and *quickest*, the *best* value and the *most* comfortable alternative so that they are the customer's choice, not you. Effective competitive strategy is defined as the strategy that wins in the contest to be the customer's choice.

Competitive strategy is most important in mature markets. In mature markets, the customers know the products; the competitors are known to the customers and to one another. Take a market like soft drinks. Coke and Pepsi are the leaders. Everyone knows it. It's not necessary to introduce customers to the idea of soft drinks. The task is to get the customers to choose one soft drink over another.

Competitive strategy is less important in emerging markets. The main task is typically to convince customers that the new products in the new market are worthy of their attention. In many cases, competing companies cooperate while the market is new to help reduce customers' anxieties and reluctance to do business.

Competitive strategy becomes more important as the market matures. Those companies that attend to their competitive strategies during the emerging market phase are better prepared to compete in a mature market.

Competitive strategy is about either being first in the minds of customers or being different from the competitor who is first. And not just any difference will do. It must be a difference that makes a difference to the customer—a difference that customers value. Furthermore, differentiated products often cost more than undifferentiated products, so the difference must generate a premium price that more than makes up for the added cost. Finally, the difference must be sustainable, not one that competitors can easily duplicate.

e-Strategy

The emerging markets of the Internet offer a wealth of strategic opportunities today. But like all strategic opportunities, these are fleeting. The Net currently offers strategic opportunities to many companies in many markets. The opportunities are based on the cost-free transfer of bits, new opportunities for relationships, quick pace of change on the Net, the dissolution of distance and network effect (we will get into them in detail later). The opportunities are so broad that every company should consider how they might take advantage of them. *e-Strategy* is the set of goals and means for achieving those goals that address the question, "How should your company take advantage of the Internet strategic opportunities?"

Effective e-Strategy

One of the characteristics of emerging markets is strategic uncertainty—it is not yet clear which are the best ways to provide value and make money. Effective strategies are obvious in established markets because the established market leaders are doing it.

As I write this, many online businesses are focusing on gaining market share in spite of high losses. The argument is that dominant market share will likely persist for decades and, as business online grows, the markets will be huge. Taking even massive losses today will seem farsighted in the future. The counter-argument is that this is simply not true, that it is a delusion created by a frenzy of investment in online ventures. Although there are strong opinions on both sides of the argument, it will truly be resolved only with time.

This book is an attempt to describe and illustrate the range of strategies being pursued today among online businesses. It is hoped that the examples and discussion provided here will help business leaders to better understand the strategic opportunities before them and to assist them in formulating their own online strategies.

Part I
Market Life Cycle

*Persistent efforts to introduce destabilizing
innovations when a young industry...is moving
toward a dominant configuration...are unlikely to
be effective. Conversely, when an industry is far
advanced in maturity, its modes of operating
and of competing become a kind of security
blanket that is increasingly vulnerable to a
destabilizing attack.*

— Lowell W. Steele, *Managing Technology*

Markets develop in a typical pattern. The stages of market development can be thought of as emerging, growing, mature, and declining. The appropriate strategies to use when addressing the market
depend upon the market's stage of development. Companies entering an emerging market have the opportunity to benefit from being
the first. Often the first into a new market is one of the dominant
players when the market is more mature and more profitable. When
in a growing market, a typical strategy is to grow quickly to establish market share. Mature markets generally have few competitors.
The dominant players in mature markets work to protect their mar-

ket share and profits while being alert to the emergence of substitute products. Declining markets require attention to controlling costs as volumes and revenues drop.

Business on the Internet is creating a collection of new markets. Just a few years into the development of commercial activity on the Internet, most of the markets are either in the emerging stage or the growing stage of market development. A few markets are mature. A very few markets are already declining.

Emerging Markets

Emerging markets are composed of first-time buyers. The market is emerging by definition because needs are being served by products that have not existed previously. Emerging markets are full of uncertainty. The most effective business strategy in an emerging market is one that is based on experimentation: experimentation with regard to products, processes and strategies. A business entering an emerging market is well advised to manage its resources under the assumption that its initial plans won't all work. A business entering an emerging market should plan on at least two or three iterations or experiments before getting it right.

The uncertainty throughout emerging markets increases business risk. However, the attraction of emerging markets is that the first businesses into an emerging market usually have a strong advantage in building market share. Dominant market share built relatively inexpensively in an emerging market may be retained by the company as the market grows to something much larger, much less risky and much more profitable.

Dominant brands tend to persist. Of the twenty-five top-selling consumer brands in the U.S. in 1960, sixteen of those are among the top-selling consumer brands in the year 2000. As companies move into emerging online markets, the ones that dominate today may well still be dominant in global online markets a half-century or more into the future.

Growing Markets

The fundamental characteristic of an emerging market is uncertainty. The transition from the emerging market stage into the growing market stage is marked by the clarification of many of the uncertainties in the marketplace. It becomes clearer how to sell to customers, which customers to sell to, which product features are most attractive, and which are the most effective strategies. With these uncertainties reduced, a wider group of buyers become interested in buying the products. Unit sales and revenues increase rapidly. The rapid increase catches the attention of many other companies who move into the growing market. As a result, companies face many more competitors than they typically would in an emerging market. With the customers' needs, products and strategies now understood, attention is turned to the problems of execution and growing market share.

Many markets on the Internet have already moved into the growing stage. The online sale of securities, the sale of business news, retail gift stores, toy stores and computer stores are in the growing stage of development. Some Internet markets such as retail book sales and CD sales have made a transition through the growing stage and are showing signs of becoming mature markets. The transition between growing markets and mature markets is usually indicated by a consolidation among the competitors down to a handful of remaining companies.

Mature Markets

Transition from growing markets to mature markets is marked by a shakeout of competitors. Competition based on price becomes more important. An increasing percentage of sales is made to repeat customers. Strategic attention is focused on retaining market share or stealing market share from competitors. The market leaders in a mature market usually enjoy high profits.

Because the population of users on the Internet continues to grow so rapidly, few online markets have reached maturity. One that has is the market for search engines. We have recently seen consolidation among the search engines with very few new companies entering the market. Fewer than a half-dozen competitors today dominate general search on the Internet. There are hundreds of specialized search engines on the Net, but these are addressing niches in the search marketplace.

In the last several years more than five thousand Internet Service Providers (ISPs) have appeared in the U.S. offering dialup access to the Internet through conventional modems. Certainly this was an example of a growing market. However, today we're seeing what appears to be consolidation in the conventional ISP market. National ISPs are gobbling up local ISPs. At the time of this writing there are still thousands of ISP's nationwide. However, their numbers are falling. Not only are they consolidating, but the ISP's that offer the new and much faster access technologies of cable modems and DSL also threaten them.

Declining Markets

Declining markets are marked by a roll-off in demand for products. The primary strategic challenge in a declining market is to control costs and keep the remaining customers as demand falls. The customers tend to be sophisticated, having used these products in earlier times. They know what they want. Companies typically spend little on research and development and little on marketing. Competitors who cannot remain profitable as volumes fall exit the market.

There are few Internet-related markets that have already moved into the declining stage, but there are some. For example, consulting and seminar services that were valued when the commercial Internet was a brand-new phenomenon are no longer in demand. There are a few takers for seminars like "Introduction to the Internet." Seminars of that type are no longer offered by industry gurus, rather by conventional training companies, the kind that might also offer courses like "Introduction to Microsoft Windows." Some technologies that were used widely on the Internet a few years ago are no longer used. Examples are Unix shell CGI scripting (replaced by Perl scripting, Active Server Pages, Cold Fusion applications and others), and Gopher information system development (replaced by the World Wide Web). As a result, consulting services for these technologies have declined or disappeared.

New Market or New Channel?

Not all the business being done on the Internet constitutes a new market. Many existing businesses have simply adopted the Internet as another channel for their existing markets. For example, semiconductor distributors now sell products through the Web. They sell those products to the same customers that they were selling to offline and the online customers have the same careabouts that they had when purchasing offline.

What about the online sale of books? Is it a new market or simply a new channel into an existing market? The questions indicate the significance of the issue. First, is that an opportunity for a new company to gain a large share of the market? Second, how large will online sales become compared to offline sales? Will online sales be a significant fraction of total sales? Of course, the example of Amazon books vs. Barnes & Noble has been dramatic and captured the attention of many online industry watchers. Amazon has captured a dominant share of online book sales. Barnes & Noble, despite vigorous effort, has been unable to overtake Amazon's lead. If the major fraction of the total national sales are transacted over the Internet in a few years, Barnes & Noble will have suffered a significant loss.

2 Emerging Markets

*The essential characteristic of an emerging
industry from the viewpoint of formulating
strategy is that there are no rules of the game.
The competitive problem in an emerging
industry is that all the rules must be established
such that the firm can cope with and prosper
under them. The absence of rules is both a risk
and a source of opportunity; in any case it must
be managed.*

— Michael Porter, *Competitive Strategy*

The last five years on the Internet have been characterized by turbulence and tumultuous change. There has been a lot of talk in the media about the high rate of change—things changing in "Internet time." This is not unusual for an emerging market. New markets are characterized by a high degree of change creating high levels of uncertainty. There's uncertainty about appropriate strategies to use, whether government and regulatory agencies will become involved and which technologies to use. Often new tools need to be developed for new applications. New standards need to be developed to ensure compatibility and interoperability.

Emerging markets are typically crowded with start-up companies. Start-up companies tend to be agile: quick to make decisions, quick to make changes as compared to their larger counterparts. This agility encourages experimentation. On the other hand, small and inexperienced companies sometimes produce products of erratic quality. One of the advantages of dealing with a large corporation is that, in most cases, the corporation grew from small to large as a result of being a dependable source of reliable products. Another characteristic of start-up companies in emerging markets is that often they lack credibility with the financial community. Internet businesses have been notable exceptions to this general rule. On the contrary, some Internet businesses have been given huge amounts of venture funding and astronomical market valuations by investors. The valuations are based not on performance, but on a wish to get in at the inception of something really big.

The customers in emerging markets are typically first-time buyers. After all, if the products in this market are brand-new, nobody has bought them before. Or maybe the products are familiar, but the experience of buying over the Net is new. First-time buyers coupled with a large proliferation of small suppliers create this situation of customer confusion. Confusion results in increased perceived risk both for customers and suppliers. Perceived risk generally means reluctance to buy.

There are no markets so new, so different, that there aren't companies that perceive the newly created businesses as encroaching on their territory. Large and established companies tend to have a lot more money to use to defend their territory than the start-up companies have to attack a territory.

Characteristics of Emerging Markets*		
External Characteristics	Businesses	Customers
Regulatory uncertainty Technological uncertainty New tools needed	Strategic uncertainty Start-up companies Agility and experimentation Erratic product quality Low credibility with financial community Responses of threatened businesses	First time buyers Customer confusion and perceived risk

Strategic Uncertainty

Strategies are well worked out in established markets. The strategies that work are the strategies that are being used by the dominant businesses. Appropriate strategies are not so clear in emerging markets. Typically, companies going into emerging markets apply the same sort of strategies that worked in similar established markets. However, it's almost always the case that emerging markets

* This analysis draws on the framework of Porter, *Competitive Strategy*.

and novel products require new strategies or at least a new spin on old strategies.

One of the early strategies for electronic commerce on the Net was to create shopping malls. The idea was to create a place in cyberspace similar to the concentration of stores in shopping malls that we find in the physical world. This is an example of a strategy brought from an existing market to a new market. But it didn't work. The advantage of shopping malls in the physical world is that they cluster businesses and make them easy for customers to find. And shopping malls effectively promote themselves simply by their physical existence. On the Net, however, any business is just a click away. Clustering per se is not necessary. With hundreds of millions of Web sites, none is promoted by its mere existence.

Making businesses easy to find on the Net is necessary. Search engines and directories became important in making online businesses easy to find. Clustering into electronic shopping malls provided no real advantage a few years ago. The electronic malls were no easier to find than the stores themselves. We do see, however, a variation on the shopping mall theme. Rather than a physical cluster of stores there are Web sites that can search for a product in many stores. Rather than a mall, these product search sites primarily operate on the buyer's behalf, allowing price comparisons across many stores.

New means of locating businesses are available online. One can search for businesses by distance from a central point. Say you're interested in hotels and restaurants within a mile of the location of a business meeting. It would have been difficult to do in the offline world, much simpler online.

What's the right strategy in an emerging market? It will have to be discovered through bright ideas and experimentation, and in the meantime uncertainty is inevitable.

Regulatory Uncertainty

What will the government do about the emerging marketplace? The Internet has held an unusually well-protected position with regard to regulation over the last five years. The Net has also been protected from new taxes. This was a conscious attempt to reduce regulatory uncertainty, thereby reducing risk and thereby encouraging investors and entrepreneurs to develop electronic commerce.

Relatively few laws regarding the Internet have been passed, in spite of popular analogies in the early commercial days of the Net as a lawless "electronic frontier." The most sweeping Internet law to date, the Communications Decency Act of 1996 was quickly struck down by the Supreme Court as unconstitutional. It's not that the Net doesn't have problems: it does. So far, the people on the Net have been left alone to solve those problems rather than have solutions dictated by lawmakers.

Businesses on the Net have been free from special sales and use taxes, although advocates have continued to lobby for them. Businesses on the Net are, of course, subject to all the laws that affect offline businesses. It has not been the case that life on the Net is a lawless electronic frontier. It is simply the case that few new laws specific to the Net have been passed.

In addition to laws, the Net has been left alone by regulators. Not that there hasn't been agitation for change. In the earliest days of Internet growth, local phone companies noticed that Internet users made local calls to their Internet Service Providers that lasted for hours, rather than the minutes of typical local calls. Many phone companies wanted to change their pricing structure to reflect these changes. As the technology for long distance voice and fax calls over the Net has become more widely used, phone companies have lobbied to change the status of Internet service, hence the pricing structure, in order to protect long distance phone service franchises. Again, as of this writing, new regulations are few and have had little effect on the Net.

What is the future of government involvement in the Net? The general assumption today is that government will do little that would stifle the Net's growth or entrepreneurial opportunities. But if that begins to change, investors and entrepreneurs will have to proceed in an atmosphere of greater risk due to the uncertainty.

Emerging markets run a particular risk from regulation in that the lawmakers and regulators are often fearful of new and powerful technologies, yet (or because) they don't fully understand them. It is sometimes the case that ill-considered laws and regulations are created out of fear when the laws aren't necessary.

Technological Uncertainty

Emerging markets are typified by technological uncertainty. Often many technologies are applied to the new problems of the new market. Some will succeed, some will fail. Widespread experimentation in new markets often results in the application of many technologies. And companies do not create the solutions alone. Most often markets and products are created jointly through the efforts and behaviors of producers and consumers. Producers imperfectly perceive customer problems and the products that will solve them. Consumers, meanwhile, discover the nuances of problems that can be addressed given the new products and technologies. It's a process involving feedback and selection.

On the Internet, some technological decisions have been made. For example, Web pages are represented in HTML (HyperText Markup Language), SSL (Secure Sockets Layer) for encrypted transactions, Adobe Acrobat for non-HTML documents and the use of Javascript for Web page scripting.

There are many technological uncertainties on the Net. Many features of Javascript, for example, cause errors and crashes when certain Web pages are displayed in different browsers and in different browser versions. Dynamic HTML works differently in some Netscape browsers than it does in some Microsoft browsers. Browsers can be expanded with plug-in applications. However, the collection of plug-ins that users have installed in their browsers varies considerably from one user to the next. Streaming audio and streaming video currently come in a variety of formats. High-speed data connections such as xDSL and cable modems are, at the time of this writing, in competition, and the dominant mode, if there will be one, is not yet clear. Other technologies, such as application locking for software downloads, have appeared but are not yet standardized or broadly used.

In time, more technologies will emerge as dominant in their application area and the competing technologies will tend to disappear. Technological uncertainty will be reduced; however, it never goes away.

New Tools Needed

New technologies require new tools. As companies experiment with new technologies and new applications in an emerging marketplace, new tools are required to facilitate the use of those new technologies.

The first seminars I conducted on creating Web pages were held in early 1994. The tool of choice was a plain text editor such as Notepad in Windows. In order to create a Web page, one had to type out all the HTML tags mixed in with the text to be displayed. Page layout was very primitive: There were no tables then, and the concept of positional page elements and cascading style sheets were years away. Only a few graphics editors could output graphics in the Compuserve GIF format required by the dominant graphical browser of the time, Mosaic. No client-side scripting, no database connections, no secure transactions. There were some tools available at that time which claimed to help but they didn't. The best tools were Notepad and patience.

In the last few years a plethora of new tools for the Internet have been developed. For example, there are HTML editors, GIF editors and GIF animators, Shockwave and Flash editors and players, development servers, ad servers, text-to-HTML converters, database-to-HTML converters, spreadsheet-to-HTML converters, Web-to-database communication tools, Web site content management tools, Web site relationship management tools, security tools, firewall tools, Java development kits, active server pages and Cold Fusion development tools. The tools still need improvement. The most commonly used tool today, Microsoft Frontpage, is notorious for making changes to Web pages, presumably to "improve" them, whether the developer wants those "improvements" or not. The tools are not yet perfect but are vastly better than they were a few years ago.

The arrival of new tools simultaneously improves the efficiency of application development and increases the number of people who are able to create applications. At the very earliest stages of an emerging market, gurus do most of the development. At later stages, improved tools enable less technologically sophisticated people to develop applications. Today there are Web sites where users can create pages simply by filling out some forms. The pages are created automatically. These pages are limited, but their virtue is that anyone who can surf the Net can create pages on these sites.

Standards Needed

With all the new technologies, new approaches and new tools, one of the most common problems of emerging markets is the lack of standards. In the early days of the railroads, railroad tracks were laid in many different gauges. The lack of standardization made it impossible for one train to ride cross-country because it could not ride on different track gauges. It was only after the standardization of track gauges that transcontinental rail traffic became possible. The same was true of the early days of the telegraph. Telegraph operators at international boundaries would receive incoming messages, then retransmit them in a different code and sometimes on a telegraph system that was electrically different from and entirely incompatible with the one the message came in on.

We see the same sort of problem today of lack of standards on the Internet. Not that there aren't a lot of standards; in fact, it's been said that the great thing about standards is that there are so many of them! But the point is to settle on one... and to adhere to it. There is a scripting standard called ECMAScript, which is a standardized version of Javascript. It's good to have a standard, but both of the major browsers, Netscape and Microsoft, have extended their Javascript-like scripting languages well beyond ECMAScript. This will settle out in time, but until then we will see a lot of pages on the Web that break due to scripts incompatible with the browsers they are being viewed on.

The Net has changed the standards situation in at least one very important way: Since software can be distributed over the Net at low cost, it can be given away for free to large numbers of users, thus creating de facto standards overnight. Many companies whose businesses depended upon being the source of a widely used standard have used this approach. It's the reason Netscape and Microsoft have given away their browsers for years, why Qualcomm gives away their basic version of the Eudora mailer and why Real gives away their streaming media players. Get lots of copies out there early, become the standard. Then your competition has to become compatible with you.

Proliferating Start-Up Companies

Start-up companies typically populate new markets. This might be surprising since new markets are difficult and expensive to establish and large companies have more money and talent to apply to establish them.

Larger, more established companies got that way because they were successful at some business. Established companies have defined missions and processes in place. The company is surrounded by opportunities, most of which lead nowhere. The more novel opportunities appear, the more likely they are to fail. As a result established companies tend to be conservative. They have found a formula that works, and they continue to apply it.

Well-managed, established companies tend to listen to their customers and do what their customers ask them to do. Typically, a market has well-defined parameters that customers care about and that companies compete to improve. In the desktop computer business, for example, customers want faster processors, more memory, more disk space and faster modems without raising prices. In fact, lower prices are appreciated.

New markets are new precisely because the customers care about different things. When palmtop computers came along, the primary careabouts were handprint recognition, weight, PC connectivity and battery life. These were not concerns with desktop PCs. Desktop PC makers and their customers couldn't care less about handprint recognition, weight and the rest. And look at the size of those markets. Customers bought billions of dollars worth of desktop PCs every year. Why should the PC makers mess with these "toy" handheld computers that their customers were not asking for? Even if they were successful, would the size of the new market be big enough? If a billion dollar business wants to grow at 10% per year, it must generate another $100 million in revenues each year. Will this new market do that or should the big company simply try to sell 10% more desktop PCs? But a start-up company could build a nice little business in a little market. Maybe it will grow to billions, maybe not. And a start-up could focus all its attention on things like handprint recognition technology, battery life and the rest. That's why new markets tend to be addressed by new companies.

New markets are typically filled with start-up companies in spite of their disadvantages. Start-up companies tend to assume greater risk. They have the advantages of providing exclusive management focus on the new markets and products to service and they are unencumbered by the baggage of success. Start-up companies don't have to figure out where the new market and products will fit into their existing product mix. Start-up companies don't have to try to make the new market seem similar to existing markets if the match really isn't there. Everything in the start-up company can be created anew for the purpose of serving the new market.

Agility and Experimentation

One of the biggest advantages of start-up companies is that there is close communication throughout the company: between the decision-makers and production, development, service, shipping, as well as between the decision-makers and customers. This greatly reduces the amount of time it takes to discover an anomaly or make a decision and to change course. Agility is very important in emerging markets. In an emerging market the best ways of doing business are just being discovered. No one yet knows the right way to do things. Therefore, experimentation is critical to success. The more quickly and cheaply a company can experiment with new products, new business models, and new ways to serve the customer the more likely that company is to succeed. This is where start-up companies have a great advantage over established companies. Because of their exclusive focus on the new marketplace and their ability to design processes specifically for the new marketplace and the short lines of communication within the start-up company, start-up businesses can move very quickly.

Because there is so much uncertainty in emerging markets, experimentation is the best strategy. Another way to look at this is that discovery is the most important attribute of businesses in emerging markets. Often, winning strategies are discovered by chance. Wal-Mart didn't start with an explicit strategy of selling in small towns, then moving to big cities when the organization was strong enough. Rather, Sam Walton's wife preferred to live in a town of fewer than 10,000. Wal-Mart's winning strategy was discovered from success. Learn whatever you can about your market and your customers. Use that knowledge to build your strategies. But in the meantime, carefully watch for what's working, where the sales and profits are really coming from. Discover what works.

A lot has been said in the media about "Internet time." Products emerge quickly, change quickly, and the fortunes of companies rise and fall quickly. This is typical of emerging markets. However, this short time frame has been reduced even further by the rapid communication between businesses and customers and among customers offered by the Internet. Yet another factor increasing the speed of change is the new economics of the Net. Web browser versions and capabilities changed every few months through the mid-1990s. Why? There were few barriers. Since new browser versions could be downloaded for free, the cost was simply the attention of the user to get around to doing it. And since the new browser features at that time were much sought after, users were motivated to take advantage of the opportunity. So browsers and their capabilities changed quickly—on Internet time.

Erratic Product Quality

Large established companies usually got that way by providing reliable products. Start-up companies are fighting against the odds and are often cash-poor. Sometimes they make the mistake of skimping on quality. In established markets low-quality providers have usually been long since run out of business. But in emerging markets the low-quality providers are mixed in with high-quality providers, resulting in a marketplace with products of erratic quality. In time the brands that supply high-quality products will be identified, and the brands that don't tend to disappear.

Is poor quality ever an acceptable approach? I say no, fully aware that many successful companies began with poor quality offerings. Sun builds powerful computers today known for their quality and reliability. However, the first Sun workstation I had access to in the early 1980s was awful. It crashed often, but it offered capabilities that were hard to find elsewhere at a comparable price. Microsoft Windows was a huge success, but not until version 3. The earlier versions were too slow to be useful, but Microsoft established its participation in the market early. Being early to market with an attractive product allows early users to overlook many problems.

First Time Buyers

It's much easier to sell a customer a product that you sold her many times before. In an emerging marketplace, nearly all the customers are first-time buyers. They don't know the companies, they don't know the products, they don't know how the products compare; they might not even be sure about how those products will address their needs. Among the greatest challenges to businesses in an emerging marketplace are to, first, get the customers' attention, second, convince them of the value of new product offerings, and, third, convince them that there is security and little risk in buying the new products. Luckily for Internet businesses the Internet itself is getting a great deal of attention. We see constant references to it in the media. Books on the Net abound. However, getting attention for a specific Web site or a specific software product can be very difficult. Many people are getting on the Web, so it's becoming easier every day to convince them of the value of Web-based products. And although it is less of a problem than it was a few years ago, there is still considerable resistance toward doing business over the Net. Many potential customers are still reluctant to enter their credit cards onto a form on a Web page.

First time customers are hard-won customers. They are costly customers to find. Strategies that deal with customer retention become especially important in emerging markets in order to reduce the cost of customer acquisition as quickly as possible. Relationship-building, customization and increasing the scope of products offered to each customer can foster repeat business. Strong referral and viral marketing programs can have a similar effect by inducing existing customers to do some of the work of locating new customers. These strategies will be discussed more fully later in the book.

Perceived Risk

An emerging market is full of start-up companies experimenting with new approaches for doing business and new types of products. In time many of these approaches and products will be found to be unsuccessful for one reason for another. They will disappear. In the meantime customers in the emerging market are exposed to a wide array of products, approaches and conflicting claims. It's no wonder that customer confusion is a typical characteristic of emerging markets. With confusion comes perceived risk. Add that to the perceived risk of the novel and the unknown, and you begin to see the reasons for strong customer resistance in emerging markets.

Established companies competing with start-ups often attempt to turn customers' perceived risk against the new companies. They often portray the familiar way as the safe way. For decades IBM dominated the computer business, a set of tumultuous markets with new products appearing continuously. IBM was notorious for selling FUD: fear, uncertainty and doubt. The saying was, no one ever got fired for choosing IBM.

Strategies for those in emerging markets who must face customer confusion and perceived risk should recognize the problem and deal with it directly. Make guarantees explicit and highly visible. Explain why the choice is safe. Simplify the offering, whether it is a product or a shopping experience, to make the customer more comfortable with it. Reassure customers with plenty of feedback: Online stores often send order confirmation e-mails, then another when the order has shipped, as well as order status and history Web pages that can provide comfort to anxious customers that all is well. If there is a problem, the best companies make strenuous efforts in customer service to make the matter right.

Financial Credibility

The typical situation in an emerging market is that the start-up companies have little credibility with the financial community. Everything about what they're trying to do is untried and unproven. That means lots of risk. And that means reluctance on the part of the financial community to provide the money necessary for companies to grow.

The situation with the Internet over the last few years has been almost exactly the opposite of the typical case of emerging markets. Investments in start-up businesses in new markets cannot ordinarily be made in the same way that investments in established companies in established markets can be made. Investments in established companies are made on the basis of analysis. What will be the return on investment? Investing in start-up companies in emerging markets cannot be done on the basis of analysis because the data simply doesn't yet exist. These investments have to be made as a bet. Electronic commerce on the Internet is seen by many to have such enormous potential in the long-term that they're willing to risk a lot to make this bet. The thinking goes something like this: let's say it's the turn-of-the-century, 1900, and you have an opportunity to invest in such businesses as Ford, AT&T, General Electric, General Motors and Standard Oil before they were enormous businesses. Wouldn't you like the opportunity to take that bet? Whether it's a good bet or not to put money on AOL, Yahoo!, or Amazon, only time will tell. However, the typical uncertainty of the financial community toward an emerging marketplace has, in the case of Internet businesses, turned into wild enthusiasm.

Wild investor enthusiasm has led to a lot of investment in businesses with poor business plans. Many e-business plans have no profits, many even have little revenue, but, worst, many have no sustainable competitive advantages. Without sustainable competitive advantage, future prospects look grim. The honeymoon with e-businesses will soon end and many of these companies will lose their market value. As I write this in April 2000, a large stock market downturn and rebound has just occurred. Many of the poorly performing e-businesses have not recovered from the downturn and may not be around much longer.

Responses of
Threatened Businesses

Emerging marketplaces typically address customer needs that have not previously been addressed. Typically, companies that have not been around before address them. However, there is no marketplace that is so remote, so different, that there are not established companies that consider the new marketplace to be rightfully part of their own. Established companies will feel threatened by the new start-up companies in the new marketplace. And they will respond. They will come at the new marketplace with more money and stronger brand recognition than the start-up companies have. For example, Apple Computer had become the leader among the start-ups for the home computer business in the early 1980s. But then along came giant IBM. It didn't take Apple's home computer business away, but it quickly dominated the much larger business PC market.

To prepare for this inevitable attack, start-up companies must establish their businesses and build connections with customers quickly, before the larger companies step in to claim what they believe is rightfully their marketplace. And the start-up companies must quickly learn and apply what they can from their advantage for experimentation within the marketplace. If the start-ups have established themselves sufficiently by the time the larger competitors arrive, the smaller companies may be able to continue to compete and even dominate the larger companies in the new marketplace. Tiny Amazon was able to create a strong online brand before giant book retailer Barnes and Noble joined in the online book business. Barnes and Noble was unable to overcome Amazon online. Furthermore,

Amazon might have had even more time to build their online brand and become even stronger before Barnes and Noble became a competitor. Amazon first appeared on Barnes and Noble's radar because of their slogan, "The World's Biggest Bookstore." Barnes and Noble thought that title rightfully belonged to them, which started legal action, then culminated in online competition. Without the slogan, Amazon might have gotten away with another year or so before Barnes and Noble came online.

Again, consider Apple. In the late 1970s, they didn't fear IBM—they feared Texas Instruments. TI had a home computer business based on a computer called the 99/4. The big difference between the Apple computer and the TI 99/4 is that Apple was open for anyone to build plug-in cards and software applications. TI tried to control software development to take more of the profits. Apple's open systems approach created more applications, so more value for customers. The TI 99/4 was discontinued after huge losses in 1983.

If the start-up has failed to establish its dominance in the market, or if the larger rival doesn't make a fatal mistake, the start-up may lose. They may choose to sell out to a larger company. Or the start-up may simply be overcome by its larger rival, become a small player, a niche player or disappear altogether.

OnlineOfficeSupplies.com (http://www.onlineofficesupplies.com) was founded in August 1998 to sell office supplies over the Net. At the time, none of the major office supply businesses sold through their Web sites. It was viewed as an opportunity to get in and establish an online brand before the big guys came in. The hope was to find Office Depot, Office Max and Staples napping just as Amazon did with the big book retailers three years before. It was risky because they all had Web sites, just not online sales. It would seem that success hinges on the ability to build one's brand very quickly.

The big brand office supply retailers did start selling online within about a year. Their very strong brand names have carried over to the online market. The OnlineOfficeSupplies.com Web site now features price comparisons with Office Depot and Office Max on their front page. Since it's unlikely that OnlineOfficeSupplies.com could have lower costs than the big brands with their volume purchases, this seems like a contest that would be very difficult to win.

There is always a threatened business and they are likely to respond. With all the media attention that online business has received, the likelihood of finding big brands ignoring online business is unlikely. Strategies must be devised that anticipate a response but can nevertheless survive.

There are strategies employed on both sides of the issue of response by threatened businesses. They will be discussed in more detail later in the book. On the new business side, companies attempt to be first to market and move quickly, establishing as strong a brand as possible before strong competitors respond. Another strategy is to use competitive judo: use the size and momentum of large competitors against them which can impede their response. On the threatened business side, creative imitation is frequently employed to follow the lead set by the innovator but outdo them at their own game.

3 Growing Markets

There is a tide in the affairs of men,
Which, when taken at the flood, leads on to
fortune;
Omitted, all the voyage of their life
Is bound in shallows and miseries.

— *Julius Caesar* by William Shakespeare

The problem of emerging markets is to convince customers that the new products actually are something of value. At the same time, the customers are teaching suppliers which product features and configurations actually solve the customers' most important problems. There is give and take and evolution until the right products are addressing the right problems at the right price. Then the growth begins.

More Customers and Volume Production

By definition, growth implies more business. Typically, the number of customers are increasing as well as quantities sold. Where small quantity production may have been sufficient in the emerging market phase, companies in a growth market typically must scale up to higher production levels.

Characteristics of Growing Markets*		
Products	Businesses	Customers
Product differentiation Good quality	Many competitors Marketing and distribution key Risks compensated by growth Mergers, acquisitions and alliances Ends with a shakeout	More customers Volume production

Online businesses in growing markets often see their traffic increase dramatically. The absolute numbers depend on the market, but at the high end, it's not unusual to see millions or tens of millions of visitors to a site per day. Since there are few impediments to access online, growth can be astonishingly fast. Free services such as Hotmail (free e-mail) and MyPoints (rewards for behavior) have seen member growth in their programs in the tens of thousands per day.

---

* This analysis draws on the framework of Porter, *Competitive Strategy*.

For precisely the same reasons that online activity can grow quickly, it can also disappear quickly. It is particularly important for e-businesses to develop strategies to retain the customers that they may acquire quickly. These are the same customer retention strategies employed in the emerging market phase.

Many Competitors

Growth tends to attract competition. New competitors may have held back during the emerging market phase or might have been completely unaware of the small emerging market. But during the growth phase the market gets hot. Lots of companies may want to get in on the growth.

This is the point where the value of sustainable competitive advantage, created during the emerging market phase, begins to demonstrate its value. Strategies based on intellectual property or exclusive partnerships with key information sources may effectively delay or preclude competitors from duplicating a business. Priceline's patent on reverse auctions has delayed others from copying the idea. Yahoo!Broadcast's exclusive partnerships for Internet broadcasts of radio stations and college sporting events has made it difficult for others to compete. Delaying competitors might be just as effective as precluding them, if it gives enough time to build dominant market share.

Product Differentiation

As more competitors appear, products tend to become more differentiated. These mutations are part of a process of market selection—a search involving customers and vendors moving together toward the most satisfactory combinations of product, price and business model.

Incremental changes are likely to be the most effective product differentiations during the growing phase of the market. This is the period when customers are just beginning to be comfortable with the products and just want the rough spots smoothed. Typically, customers are not looking for a radically new approach. A strategy that provides customized products is particularly attractive. By allowing customers to pick and choose among a large collection of options, the seller gets immediate feedback with each order on which options are preferred and which are not. The same customer preference information can feed up the supply chain, helping component builders and designers respond more quickly. Customization has been a successful strategy for Dell and Gateway in the computer business.

Another mechanism that can accelerate the process of differentiation and market selection is encouraging feedback. Magazine-like sites, for example, often provide quick feedback forms asking how useful each article is. Each article on the *Business 2.0* site (http://www.business2.com) includes a floating menu asking the reader to rate how useful she found the page. The more immediate the feedback, the quicker a business can tune its offering to the needs and preferences of its customers.

Good Quality

Poor quality may be tolerated in the emerging market phase. Everyone knows there are bugs to be worked out; and, besides, there are few alternatives. But as the customer base expands and volumes increase, quality becomes an imperative. Said another way, if quality remains poor, an emerging market may simply fizzle out, never reaching the growth phase.

In the early days of search engines they were often unusable. They could not sustain the traffic loads they experienced. This was in part due to the fact that they didn't have any source of income. The early search engines were labors of love or university student projects implemented on whatever server was handy. As they became more widely used, they bogged down. Then came venture funding and advertising revenues. Now there was money to invest in greater server capacity and higher bandwidth connections to the Net. Quality improved to the point that today search engines and directory sites are among the most responsive sites on the Net, in spite of the huge amounts of traffic they serve.

High quality may not be an effective competitive advantage in mature markets; it may simply be a requirement of being in business. High quality may, however, be a competitive advantage during the growth phase of the market. If early products in the market have been characterized by poor reliability, the first company to establish itself as the high quality provider may be the first to earn large volume purchases, which could result in early market share advantages.

Quality in online businesses is often reflected in such features as Web site speed, no dead links, an absence of fancy Java or Javascript features that unexpectedly break, responses to "contact us" messages and frequent feedback to assure customers that their orders are being handled promptly and correctly. Often companies forego elaborate designs in favor of conservative designs that are more reliable.

Marketing and Distribution Key

A corollary of increasing customer base is that more customers must be reached. They must be made aware of the products and gain access to them. Thus marketing and distribution become much more important than they were in the emerging market phase.

The search engines were among the first volume businesses on the Web, and they all depended on various forms of advertising for their revenues. In 1997-1998 a strange thing was happening. The ad revenues of the major sites, mostly search engines, were increasing. That sounded good—until one examined the list of heavy advertisers. Many of the heaviest advertisers were the very same companies that were selling ad space!

Distribution of information products across the Net is simple and cheap. The business of selling downloadable software has very low overhead. It's complicated somewhat by the issue of returns (because the customer still has the bits he's returning) and piracy, but distribution of bits is otherwise pretty simple. However, most of online business is actually about physical product, in which case distribution becomes quite challenging. Many online businesses start off with a virtual inventory model. The online retail store holds no physical inventory but simply passes orders on to a distributor for fulfillment. Amazon started with practically no inventory but located itself next to one of the largest book distributors, Ingram. Orders were passed to Ingram, packed up and taken to Amazon, repacked for shipping, then sent off. Early on, in the emerging phase, this inefficiency was tolerable. As volumes grew in the growth phase of the online book market, Amazon had to create its own warehousing and distribution facilities to cut costs and remain competitive with new entrants to the market such as Barnes and Noble.

In online businesses involving physical goods, distribution can become essential to the success of the business. Although shopping online is convenient, two of the biggest negatives are the cost and delays of shipping—both elements of distribution. We are seeing a lot of experimentation today with distribution. Many companies offer free shipping to encourage sales. Others ship overnight. Some maintain stock at the hubs of overnight shippers so that orders placed in the late afternoon or evening will still arrive anywhere in the country early the next day. Still others, like Outpost.com (http://www.outpost.com) offer same day delivery. Orders in by 9 am are delivered by 6 pm on the same day (for a hefty fee). Same day delivery is accomplished not just by stocking at shippers' hubs, but by stocking in major cities. Same day delivery is available only in those cities.

Risks Compensated
by Growth

There are risks in a rapidly growing marketplace. Uncertainty remains about the best strategies and technologies. New competitors
appear, disrupting plans. Strategic experiments are run in the search
for robust business models. Mistakes are made. But the nice thing
about a market in the growth phase is that there is more money
available tomorrow to help pay for mistakes made today.

One risk that is caused by growth can be addressed with the new
technology. Growth typically requires a lot of cash. Parts must be
bought today to build products for tomorrow. However, in a rapidly
growing market, the cash generated from sales today may not be
sufficient to pay for the larger volume of parts required for tomorrow's
higher sales volumes. The result is negative cash flow and is often
the cause for problems and failures even as markets boom and prospects seem at their best. As we will discuss later, tighter information
integration among manufacturers, suppliers and customers can reduce or even eliminate the cash flow problem caused by rapid growth.

Mergers, Acquisitions
and Alliances

Many competitors appear in growing markets; but, typically few will
survive. Some markets remain fragmented because there is no
particular economy of scale, no compelling reason for companies to
join forces. However, the more common case is that there are econo-

mies of scale. Companies with larger market shares are able to provide their services at lower cost than smaller competitors can.

The search engines were busy with mergers, acquisitions and alliances through 1998 and 1999. For example, Yahoo! acquired Four11, Viaweb, WebCal, Yoyodyne Entertainment, Hyperparallel, Geocities, Broadcast.com and Arthas.com. At the same time Lycos acquired FamilyTime.com, Shopexpert.com, Valent, Gamesville.com, Quote.com, Sonique, Wired Digital, Guestworld, Tripod, WiseWire and GlobeComm. Both companies entered into many partnerships, alliances and strategic investments with other companies to expand their market share and the breadth of their offerings.

Shakeout

When rapid growth slows, as it inevitably does, the number of vendors in a market typically falls to a handful, usually about five major competitors. The companies that have been unable to build a strong customer base disappear from the market through merger, acquisition, refocus or going out of business. As of this writing shakeouts have not been apparent in online markets. It is clear that they will.

Part II
Strategic Themes:
How the Net is Different

Dorothy: Toto, I have a feeling we're not in Kansas anymore.

— from *The Wizard of Oz*

Online business differs from offline business in several important ways. Following are five strategic themes that run through successful online businesses.

- The New Economics of the Net

- New Relationships of the Net

- New Timing

- The Dissolution of Distance

- Network Effects

Most successful online businesses use some combination of these five strategic themes.

4 New Economics

*Download Internet Explorer 5.01—the newest
version of Internet Explorer with 56-bit encryption!*

— Microsoft.com, free software
distribution calls for new strategies

The cost of moving bits around on the Net is zero. It's not cheap; it's
free!* Once you have a connection to the Net there's no additional
charge for moving bits around. That is the basis of the New Economics of the Net.

Id Software has developed several of the most successful computer
games of all time. One of the first of these was a game called Doom.
When Id developed Doom, they had a very limited marketing bud-
get, so they used the new economics of the Net. The idea was to
build Doom in three levels: level 1, level 2 and level 3. They would
make level 1 available for free to anyone who wanted to download it
over the Net. They announced in the gaming discussion groups that
they had a great new game and that anyone who wanted to download it could do so. And they could share it with their friends. They

---

* Okay, it's not free. It's billed on a flat rate model rather than a
metered (pay-per-bit) model. The result of flat rate pricing is that
the incremental cost of each bit or Web page or file is zero.

called their strategy drug dealer marketing. It worked like this: After you tried level 1 for free, you'd *have to have* level 2 and level 3, and you'd be willing to pay for them. The strategy worked. Thousands of copies of level 1 were downloaded and shared, which generated tens of millions of dollars worth of sales of level 2 and level 3. What did these tens of millions of dollars worth of sales of level 2 and level 3 cost Id Software? Distribution cost? Zero. Bits can be moved for free. The promotion was done through discussion groups. There's no cost for participating in discussion groups. Inventory cost? Zero. So, from the zero promotion cost, zero distribution cost and zero inventory cost, Id Software created tens of millions of dollars worth of sales. The New Economics of the Net.

When building a business on the Net, consider incorporating the Net's intrinsic advantages into the offering. And consider the advantages of adjacent technologies. eOriginal (http://www.eoriginal.com) is an example.

eOriginal's business is executing and storing digitally signed documents. Businesses can create the electronic equivalent of a negotiable "blue-ink-signed" original document. The process makes it possible to complete business transactions over the Internet by creating unique and secure electronic originals, eliminating the need for paper documents.

Send them in over the Net (use free Net transfer). Realize that the adjacent technology of storage is continuing to plummet in cost—storage will not be costly. And the adjacent technology of digital signatures is available and inexpensive. On top of this, place a

service that allows clients to produce authenticated copies of important electronic documents, highly valued if disputes should arise.

Netscape and the
New Economics

Mosaic, the first graphical Web browser, was developed by graduate
students at the University of Illinois. They made it available for free
across the Net and it was an instant hit: millions of copies were
downloaded, it was talked about in all sorts of publications, from
technical trade magazines to the *Wall Street Journal* and everybody
loved it. Soon the developers must have thought, if only I had a
dollar for each copy of Mosaic, I'd be doing okay now. So they formed
a company, Netscape, to do just that.

But here's the strategic challenge: how to compete with a product
that has nearly 100% market share, is the darling of the press, is
loved by everybody and is *free*? Netscape made good use of the
New Economics of the Net.

How to compete? The typical answer from a developer would be,
build a better browser! But a technically superior product is rarely
sufficient to unseat a dominant product...unless the replacement is
very superior.

The answer from Netscape (and as we all know, the strategy worked),
was to use the New Economics of the Net. With physical products it's
expensive to buy market share by giving away product. Obviously,
each one given away costs something. But not so with information

products across the Net. They can be given away at effectively zero incremental cost per copy. But Netscape's strategy went beyond this.

Netscape used a paired product strategy: They offered both new client software (the browser) and new server software. And the key differentiator was that if a Netscape browser was talking to a Netscape server, the transactions between them could be encrypted. Netscape aggressively pushed the notion that encrypted transactions would foil would-be credit card thieves.

Ordinary transactions going across the Net are sent in the clear, meaning that it is possible for a skilled systems administrator to look at transactions and messages passing through her systems as they traverse the Net. If she can look at them she could write a program to scan them as they go by—scan them, for example, for anything looking like credit card numbers. So if hackers were going to set up credit card number sniffing programs with the intent to capture and abuse the card numbers, electronic commerce would be inhibited.

Along comes Netscape and encrypted transactions, making it vastly more difficult to crack the encryption than the value of having a stolen credit card number. The Net with encrypted transactions is seen to be safe for electronic commerce.

And by the way, the Netscape browser also happened to be better than the Mosaic browser.

So the free downloads of the Netscape browser began. People wanted to get in on those encrypted transactions. The more Netscape browsers were out there (enabled for encrypted transactions), the greater the demand for Netscape servers, the only servers at the time which could handle encrypted transactions. The more Netscape servers (which Netscape sold), the greater the demand for Netscape browsers.

The paired product strategy worked. Netscape browsers soon displaced Mosaic browsers. Netscape grew on the basis of server sales. But the strategy of giving away literally millions of free copies of the Netscape browser can only work with the New Economics of the Net: the fact that information can be given away at almost zero incremental cost.

One more interesting point: There never was and still isn't a single recorded case of a credit card number being stolen and abused as it crossed the Internet, encrypted or not.

Improving Products
at No Cost

I recently had a computer crash, after which my mouse stopped working. I figured I'd try installing a new driver for the mouse so started looking all over the house for the floppy disks with drivers that came with the mouse. After several minutes of fruitless search, I realized I was doing it all wrong. Why look all over the house for those floppy disks when I could go to the Logitech Web site and download new drivers immediately? So I typed www.logitech.com into my browser, selected the mice and trackball support page, clicked on my mouse type and downloaded and installed the latest driver. It fixed my broken mouse problem. What did it cost Logitech? They had to create the Web site, but the incremental cost to Logitech for me to download the driver was zero. In return they have a customer using their product more effectively than I could have otherwise.

Dell Computer takes this idea even further. Dell collects their customer support experience into a large knowledge base of troubleshooting information, documentation and other support files that help keep the millions of computers they sell running and useful. Most companies keep their customer support knowledge for the use of their support people only. However, many forward-looking companies, like Dell, make all of their customer support information available through their Web site. Customers can do their own troubleshooting and problem-solving using exactly the same information that their customer support people would use. In many cases, customers can solve problems more quickly themselves than if they involve a customer support agent. What does it cost Dell to distribute this information to the customers and thereby provide better service? They are collecting the information for their customer support people regardless of whether it's made available over the Web or not. So the incremental cost of creating the information is zero. The cost for each customer to access the information is also zero. Better customer service at zero cost. The New Economics of the Net.

The New Economics of the Net applies to all kinds of bits, including e-mail. TI&ME is a personalized view of the Texas Instruments Web site (http://www.ti.com) that I implemented for them in 1995. TI has a large number of products and a large number of customers, but each customer is interested in only a very small number of TI's products. TI&ME is a system to personalize the TI Web site to high-

light those product areas of most interest to each individual customer. The customer registers with TI&ME and specifies his interests. Then when he visits the TI Web site, he is presented with a
personalized page showing what's new in his areas of interest. In
addition, he can elect to receive a weekly e-mail that highlights the
latest happenings in his interest areas. The customer benefits from
timely information delivered directly to his e-mail account. TI benefits by keeping in touch with customers who have expressed interest in the information. Do the customers find it valuable? There are
currently over 110,000 TI&ME members—a strong indication that
many do find it valuable. There was a cost to TI to create the
system, but the weekly cost of sending 110,000 customized messages to interested customers is zero. The New Economics of the
Net applied to e-mail.

Low Transaction Costs

The Net makes communication cheaper and easier, just as telephones
and faxes do. But the Net has computers on the sending and receiv-
ing ends of those communications, which makes it possible for transactions to be cheaper and easier as well. Those transactions may be
simple and low-level, such as the messages and acknowledgements
that go on to successfully route and move an e-mail message from
my computer in Dallas to yours, wherever in the world it may be
located.

Transactions may be higher-level, like when you buy an item from
an online store with a credit card. If you want to buy a book online,
you may first search for booksellers at a directory site like Yahoo!.

Yahoo! links you to many booksellers such as Amazon, Barnes and Noble and lots of specialty bookstores. You click on Amazon and then search the site for the kinds of books you want. You review the options, read their synopses, look at the reviews and eventually make a decision. If you are a frequent Amazon customer, you may have 1-Click Ordering enabled. If so, you click a button and the rest of the transaction is done behind the scenes.

Typical behind the scenes online order processing goes like this. The order and the customer's name, address and credit card information is captured. (With 1-Click Ordering, the customer's ID number is stored in a cookie on his computer. The Web site retrieves the cookie, uses the ID number to look up his name and credit card info in a database.) At most sites, however, it's done through filling out a form. The browser encrypts the sensitive information on the form before it's sent to the server. Encryption requires its own set of transactions. The browser requests an encryption key from the server, which the server sends. The browser uses that key to encrypt the message and sends it back to the server. The only way to decrypt the message is to use another key, paired with the first, which is stored on the server. The server decrypts the message and must now verify the credit card.

The store's server contacts a credit card processing company's server, which will look up the credit card number, verify that it is valid, and check that the purchase does not exceed the card's credit limit. Again, these communications back and forth are encrypted, so similar encryption transactions are performed. If all is okay with the card, the purchase transaction is authorized and the order is sent on to fulfillment, perhaps Amazon's book warehouse in Nevada. There the book is picked from stock and mailed to the customer. If the book weren't in stock (which would be determined by checking the warehouse inventory database), the fulfillment message would be sent on to a distributor.

The point is, for a simple online book purchase, a lot of activity is occurring behind the scenes. And in reality, many more transactions occur than what I have listed here. But networked computers make transactions very inexpensive. The cost advantage of transactions on the Net is one of the important elements of the New Economics of the Net.

Costs of transactions

Transaction costs can be broken down into costs for six kinds of activities: searching, information gathering, bargaining, decision-making, policing and enforcing agreements.

Searching. One of the first applications on the Web continues to be one of the most widely used: search engines. Imperfect as they are, search engines make it much easier to find companies and products on the Net than it would be to find them in the offline world. One can search directories like Yahoo! for company names or Web page indices like Hotbot, Lycos, Infoseek and Excite for product names or product descriptions. More specialized shopping search engines such as Excite Shopping (http://shopping.excite.com), GO Shopping (http://shop.go.com) or Yahoo!Shopping (http://shopping.yahoo.com) allow one to search hundreds of online stores simultaneously. This makes the customer's search costs dramatically lower than calling or visiting a large number of stores in the offline world. Savings are realized at least in the customer's time if not also travel and other costs.

Information gathering. Once a shopper has located possible products and where to buy them, she typically collects information about the product alternatives and the store alternatives in preparation for making a buying decision. Again, the Net dramatically lowers costs, typically in time. Some retail sites specialize in the information-gathering step of purchase transactions.

We may each have personal software agents someday which work on our behalf and seek out the products we most want at the best prices available. Some companies are already doing business on that idea but without having to create "personal agents." Many commerce sites such as Netmarket (http://www.netmarket.com) thrive based on a large variety of products and excellent systems for side-by-side comparisons.

When buying a product at Netmarket, you select a product category and then choose the product features that are important to you. Netmarket creates a table of matching products for you to compare and contrast. You can narrow your search, then buy the one that best fills your needs.

Many companies make product information available for gathering—both companies in business-to-consumer markets and business-to-business markets. Texas Instruments produces over 10,000 semiconductor products. The products are complex and design engineers need access to accurate part specifications to consider designing them into electronic applications. TI, like many companies, makes its product specs available over the Net, easily available to informa-tion-gathering design engineers. The engineers get easy access to the information they need, and it is the most up-to-date informa-tion. And it saves TI a lot of money. Before the Net, specs were distributed on paper, either spec sheets or in data books. The aver-age cost to TI of mailing out a requested technical document is $6. So, whenever a tech document is downloaded from TI's Web site, it's equivalent to a $6 cost avoidance. With the rate of tech docu-ment downloads over the Web, TI's current cost avoidance is counted in millions of dollars each week.

Bargaining. Fixed price retailing was introduced with the advent of large department stores in the mid-1800s. It was largely a practical matter. Bargaining was feasible in small stores where the customer was dealing with the owner or someone close to him. The sales-people were, of course, authorized to bargain with the customers for the best deal they could get. When large department stores came along, it was no longer feasible to entrust an issue as critical to business as pricing to thousands of low paid sales clerks. Fixed price retailing was introduced and was an instant success.

Not only did fixed price retailing eliminate the stress of bargaining for each and every item purchased, but it was cheaper. It was cheap and easy for the customers and cheap and easy for the retailers. It spread quickly throughout retailers, large and small. Bargaining was reserved in the United States for a small number of expensive purchases: homes, automobiles and sometimes jewelry.

Fixed price retailing doesn't work well for unique items. It is hard to know what to charge for a baseball signed by Babe Ruth, for example. Auctions have been popular for selling one of a kind items, in spite of the extra time (higher transaction cost) that an auction demands. Enter online auctions like eBay (http://www.ebay.com) for consumer collectibles, eSteel (http://www.esteel.com) for steel and Altrade (http://www.altraenergy.com) for commercial electricity, natural gas and liquids. Suddenly, the cost of bargaining is significantly lower due to these online markets.

Will fixed-price retailing disappear? It's unlikely to happen anytime soon, but we are already seeing a lot of experimentation with pricing online in addition to auctions. Airlines offer special low fares to customers who can fly within the next few days—made possible by the quick and inexpensive communication across the Net. Priceline (http://www.priceline.com) offers a form of reverse auctions: The customer names his price for air travel, then Priceline works to find an airline who will offer the travel for that price or less. (Priceline keeps the difference.)

Pricing could be adjusted in real time based on demand. This is exactly what an auction is about, but what about sales for mass-produced items? Consider the recent cases of Christmas toy crazes, Tickle Me Elmo, Beanie Babies and Furbys. Manufacturers forecast demand, build for the forecast, and then see how holiday buying shapes up relative to the forecast. If the forecast was too high, money is lost as unsold inventory. If it's low, potential revenues are lost. In recent years, the hot holiday toys have appeared on eBay and sold at prices ten times or more the original price. Speculators pocket the difference, not the manufacturer. But what if the manufacturer were getting real time feedback on toy sales? First, there might be time to adjust production. Second, prices could be adjusted, aimed at selling the available stock, no more and no less. Real time feedback accomplishes much the same thing as an auction.

Decision-making. Let's say you have two opportunities to buy a Rolex watch: from a shady-looking character who approaches you on the street in New York or from Tiffany's. You will make your buying decision on your ability to ascertain the authenticity of the watch, the reputation of the seller, and possibly other factors such as immediate availability, return policy, acceptance of credit cards or cash only and so on. The issue comes up in retailing but is even more critical in business-to-business transactions, which are typically of higher value. The buyer must assure himself of the seller and his product while the seller must assure himself of the creditworthiness of the buyer.

The most common approach to speed up this process (i.e., reduce this element of transaction cost) is branding: working with sellers you know and trust. There is a rush today by companies with well-known and trusted brands to do business on the Internet. However, in many cases, they are being beaten to the market by new, online-only stores. Amazon is the most famous example of an online brand beating the established offline brands to the online market. The cost of decision-making has probably increased for some online transactions with the emergence of new, unknown online vendors.

Some attempts have been made to assure online shoppers of the dependability of unfamiliar vendors. An early concern was credit card security. Credit card theft was perceived to be a significant risk of online purchases. In order to offer some assurance, Mastercard created the Shop Smart! program, which authorizes online shops to display the Shop Smart! logo if the site conforms to the best online retailing practices (i.e., whether the site encrypts credit card numbers as they cross the Net.)

With all the new businesses popping up on the Web, potential customers often have questions about the reputation of sellers that go beyond credit card security. BizRate (http://www.bizrate.com) addresses those questions. Vendors can put the BizRate icon on their site, inviting customers to rate the business. Customers can click on the button to rate the business or see the results of past ratings. Businesses are given an overall rating as well as more specific ratings for ease of ordering, product selection, product information, price, on-time delivery, customer service and other aspects of the business. The count of surveys is included to give an idea of the statistical significance of the results. (BizRate is free to vendors and free to customers. It contains no ads. Nice service, but how do they make money? BizRate uses the statistics coming in on businesses from all over the Web as the basis for online business research reports, which they sell. So, the whole service is free with BizRate making money off the "by-product" information.)

Policing. Did the buyer pay? Did the seller deliver? Keeping track of promises made and kept is part of the transaction cost. Essential to policing transactions is maintaining an audit trail. This is another area where online transactions excel. Common practice in online stores is to present a confirmation Web page of the purchase, which the buyer is urged to print for his records. It's followed by a confirmation e-mail describing the purchase and perhaps listing the terms and conditions of sale. That may be followed by an additional e-mail notifying the customer that the order has been shipped. Finally, many retailers offer online order histories through their Web sites, which spell out the details of all past transactions between a customer and the store. And why not provide all this? The Web pages, generated e-mails and order histories can be provided at essentially no cost per transaction, once the systems are set up.

Enforcing agreements. If something goes wrong with online transactions, enforcing the agreement is essentially the same as mail order sales in the offline world. There is no particular online cost advantage except the advantage of better audit trails, which would tend to reduce somewhat disputes and the need for enforcement.

Coordination through inexpensive transactions

Electronic links between online businesses and their wired suppliers make it possible to integrate the supply chain at a very low cost per transaction. Online stores can keep track of suppliers' inventory levels in real time, eliminating the possibility of offering products for sale to customers that cannot be fulfilled. Similarly, suppliers can get real time updates on the sale of their products down the supply chain through retail sales. Real time supply information was pioneered before the Internet using electronic data interchange (EDI) through costly proprietary networks. Today the Net is being used as a very low cost shared networking infrastructure, eliminating the dependence on expensive proprietary networks. At the same time, the connection protocols between buyers and sellers are being simplified, making it easier and cheaper for companies to get started in electronic supply chain integration. Costs come down, delays are reduced or eliminated and the roles of some steps in the supply chain need to be reconsidered.

Fossil, the maker of watches and apparel, sells most of their product through distributors and large department stores. They have EDI connections to these major partners. But they also sell to specialty stores (as well as retail customers) through their Web site. The Web site sales has made working with specialty stores much more efficient for both parties. In the past, specialty stores would order from catalogs. Some items could be out of stock; others may have been discontinued. Product availability is reflected in the online catalog, virtually eliminating the problem of delayed or unfillable orders. In addition, all manual order processing has been automated through Web orders, eliminating transcription errors and delays.

Garden.com offers over 20,000 gardening products but stocks almost none of them. All orders are filled through close backend integration with suppliers. When an order comes into Garden.com, it is immediately passed on to a supplier to be shipped.

It would be impractical for Garden.com to stock inventory. The many thousands of live goods offered cannot be warehoused. They would die. This is why no gardening superstores have emerged in the offline world. But online electronic connections and the inexpensive transactions of the Net make an online gardening superstore like Garden.com possible.

When an order is placed at Garden.com, it is electronically passed to the various growers who will fill the order. Garden.com monitors the growers' real time inventories of all the products it offers. That way it can ensure that any product offered through the Garden.com Web site can be fulfilled in spite of the fact that it carries no inventory itself.

Cisco Systems builds routers, specialized computers used in making computer networks. About 80% of the orders coming into Cisco come in through their Web site (http://www.cisco.com). The site assists customers in selecting the kinds of features a router would need for the customer's application. Then the orders are checked by software to ensure that necessary components are included in the order. Once the order is complete, it typically gets forwarded to one of nearly forty factories that are run by contract manufacturers, not by Cisco. The contract manufacturers, in many cases, complete the assembly of the routers and send them direct to the customer. Cisco does not touch the finished product. Contract manufacturing saves Cisco between $500 million and $800 million per year.

How can Cisco outsource such a critical part of its business? By keeping very close tabs on the operation. And that is done through tight coordination through information. Cisco designs the manufacturing process used at each of its contract manufacturing sites, then monitors the production process through real time data transmitted through the Net. The data collection and process management is a series of transactions. This degree of integration with a contractor is made possible by the low cost of transactions across the Net.

Why do a dozen roses from Proflowers (http://www.proflowers.com) cost $10-$20 less than from other online florists? Proflowers sells their flowers direct from the grower. Not only are they less expensive, but they also tend to be a couple of days fresher than flowers that have gone from grower to warehouse to florist to consumer.

It used to be, if you were a mortgage banker looking for loan money, you'd have to receive and shuffle through a pile of faxes of loan tables. Not anymore. Today, at IMX Exchange (http://www.imx.com) you can post your needs and have lenders bid for your business. It's not unusual for a broker to save a half point on the loan and another half point for the homebuyer he serves. Better information, better deals.

Many tasks are simply cheaper to perform on the Net, due to ubiquitous connections to vast amounts of information. For example, Humana (http://www.humana.com) had paid an average of $128 per qualified applicant in its recruiting effort. It then turned to the resumes found online where it scanned and filtered them automatically then matched them to current job openings and it e-mails candidates for updates to their resumes. Current average cost per qualified candidate? Six cents!

The cost of executing a transaction over the Net is very low. Omni Hotels pays travel agents $20 to make a reservation. That's about 10% of a one-night stay. But now Omni can take registrations through its Web site for about fifty cents. A factor of 40 change in the economics of reservations is bound to change the relationship between hotels and travel agents. It's bound to change the industry.

Computer-mediated communication can depersonalize conversation. Usually, that's a deficit to overcome, but CyberSettle (http://www.cybersettle.com) is based on exactly that. A common impediment to settling lawsuits is that personalities get in the way. CyberSettle provides a mechanism for the parties in a dispute to each register three offers of what they would be willing to settle for. It then compares pairs of offers, one from each side, and if they match (or are within the parameters of being close enough), the case settles. If they don't match, the offers made are not revealed to the other side so bargaining positions for future negotiations have not been damaged.

CyberSettle charges a variety of fees for these services, which they claim are far lower than typical fees off the Net. The defendant (usually an insurance company) is charged an initial fee to place a claim on the system and then an engagement fee when the claimant attorney enters demands. A settlement fee is then charged both the insurance company and the attorney when the case settles. The attorney is typically charged $200, and this fee is deducted from the settlement check before it is sent to the attorney. Volume discounts are available.

Ronald Coase was awarded the Nobel Prize in Economics in 1991 in part for describing how the size of companies is determined by transaction costs. The idea is that for any product or service a company uses, it can produce the product or service itself or buy it on the open market. Transaction costs of buying from the open market are compared to the added costs of producing the product in-house, costs collectively referred to as bureaucracy. Should the company stock its own office supplies or have each employee search, gather information, decide on price, make a buying decision, and so on? The transaction costs are compared to the price of a pen or some staples. But what about manufacturing? What about warehousing and distribution? As transaction costs come down, it makes sense to outsource more of the tasks of a company. Lower transaction costs suggest smaller companies. And that is what we are seeing in the United States: Amid continuing announcements of downsizing of large corporations, unemployment is near record low levels. The economy is not losing jobs, it is shifting them from large corporations to smaller businesses. It is redistributing work from integrated corporations to networks of coordinated companies doing the work more efficiently.

When people speak of the Net as creating "frictionless" commerce, the elimination of transaction costs is what they are talking about. Transaction costs are the friction. The Net will not eliminate all the friction. However, there is a lot of potential to reduce economic friction, enough potential to change the way companies organize to do business. The shift in organizational structure from large integrated companies to networks of smaller coordinated companies may bring about some of the most significant social changes that the Net is likely to generate.

How far will it go? Staples (http://www.staples.com) and Office Depot (http://www.officedepot.com) both offer companies the opportunity to outsource their office supplies by putting a customized office supply store on the company intranet. Employees can access the intranet store, order the items they are authorized to order and have them delivered to their desks. The online intranet office supply stores reduce transaction costs to an extent that competes with the department supply cabinet.

Services from inexpensive computing resources

Computing resources are cheap and getting cheaper all the time. Disk space, processing cycles, e-mail service and so on, it's all pretty cheap. In fact, so cheap that many companies give it away either to draw an audience for advertising or to draw attention to other services performed for a fee.

If content brings traffic, how do you create content? The GeoCities answer is, let someone else do it. GeoCities (now part of Yahoo! at http://geocities.yahoo.com) gives away space to create free Web sites. The sites are organized into "neighborhoods" according to their content. The people getting the free Web sites create content and promote it, if they feel like it. GeoCities pops up ads when the Web sites are visited.

Let's say you want to make a business out of helping customers maintain their Web sites. You have software that will check server speed, look for broken links, bad HTML, stuff like that. How do you build the business? Give the service away!

NetMechanic (http://www.netmechanic.com) allows anyone to run server checks, link checks, HTML checks and more for free. It's very useful but it's limited. If you're really serious about your site maintenance, NetMechanic hopes you'll subscribe to the service for constant monitoring. It costs NetMechanic only processing time to give away the free service; but by doing so, they demonstrate their capabilities to a broad audience.

Free or Fee?

One of the attractive characteristics of information is that using it does not use it up. When you buy a computer, you have it and no one else does. Pricing of computers and other physical products is based on answering the question, who is going to get it? But bits are different. If I have some digital information, software, documents, images, whatever, I can give you a copy and still have the information myself. I can make lots of copies, and so can you, for that matter. The cost of copying is negligible, so what should copies cost? If digital information were priced on the basis of the cost of making copies, as most physical goods are, it would all be free. But one must at least recoup the cost of development. The opportunity to distribute bits for free is creating new business models.

Pricing decisions have been made as long as there has been commerce. One of the most famous examples is King Gillette's decision to sell his safety razor at a fraction of the cost to produce it in order to sell blades. When first introduced, the razor cost the better part of a week's income for a typical working man. It severely limited the market. But by selling the razor well below cost, Gillette created demand for the blades, which were inexpensive but had to be replaced nearly every day, as long as the razor was used. The pricing strategy was an enormous success.

Another familiar example is Perrier bottled water. Sales were poor until the price was raised, positioning Perrier as a premium product. Sales took off.

So, what should one charge for information products? They may be downloaded for free like Microsoft's Internet Explorer browser. Or one may download an electronic version of a different product, Microsoft Office, from an online store at a cost of over $600. The difference isn't in the bits: it's in the pricing strategy. The New Economics of the Net creates lots of options for creative pricing.

One of the common motivations for distributing software for free is to grab market share to become the standard platform. For example, Netscape's early free browser generated demand for Netscape servers in order to take advantage of secure transactions between browser and server.

One of the best ways to sell a product is to put it in the prospect's hands. With software downloads you can do that worldwide for virtually no cost. Many software products are given away for free in order to create demand for enhanced versions. Id Software gave away Doom, level 1, which created demand for levels 2 and 3. Qualcomm gives away the basic version of its Eudora mail software, which creates demand for upgrades and the more advanced Eudora Pro. Software is downloadable for free in demonstration versions, which are typically fully operational for a limited time period. The demo can be converted to fully functional software by purchasing an activating password.

Many companies give away information on their Web sites to improve sales and service. Texas Instruments avoids the cost of mailing out paper product specifications on integrated circuits. FedEx avoids the cost of fielding phone calls by making package-tracking information freely available through their Web site.

With all the opportunity to give away information for free, the motivation is usually that someone makes money somewhere along the line. If a site offers information sufficiently interesting to draw a crowd, advertising to the crowd through the site may pay off. A few very busy sites and some highly specialized sites are quite profitable from ad revenues. Most smaller, less focused sites, however, have difficulty generating much revenue from ads.

When the commercial Internet appeared in 1994-1995, many thought that an important element of success would be subscriptions, much like the business model of magazines and newspapers. Subscription revenues have been less common than was first expected, largely due to the vast amount of free information available over the Net. The *Wall Street Journal* (http://www.wsj.com) has been successful with subscriptions largely due to its very strong brand as a premier source for business news.

More common are partly free, partly subscription sites like *Business Week* (http://www.businessweek.com). The most common value proposition for subscription sites is quality. The notion of quality is usually expressed through brand recognition. The *Business Week* site offers access to some current articles for free, but most of the articles and all of the archives require an annual subscription fee, which I gladly pay. I know the kind of information I'll find there and I'm comfortable with the level of quality. In addition, I know that most of my executive clients read *Business Week*, so before I present to them I want to know what they've been exposed to. And the reason I subscribe to the Web site but not the paper magazine: I hate having all those magazines piling up around the house!

The ESPN Sportzone site (http://www.espn.com) provides a vast amount of free sports information. For some fans that's not enough. The most avid fans can subscribe to access even more sports information. Some columnists are available only through the subscription portion of the site, not anywhere else on the Net. Like the *Wall Street Journal*, much of the information on the ESPN site is generated by ESPN so it can't be found elsewhere on the Net.

The *New York Times* (http://www.nytimes.com) is one of the best-known newspapers in the world. News, opinions and prestige. Out of all they offer, what is most valuable? What are people willing to pay an online subscription fee for? Crossword puzzles. Readers can see the entire issue of the *New York Times* online for free (subsidized by advertising, of course), except for the crossword puzzles. The puzzles cost $9.95/year. Hmm.

The highest revenues on the Net are being generated by transactions, companies selling products and services to consumers and especially to other companies (revenues from business-to-business sales are currently about 5 times higher than business-to-consumer sales.) The short answer to the question, how do you make money on the Net, is "sell." Use the New Economics of the Net to support those sales.

Let's say you have a software product, a 3D modeling package. What are you going to do with your Web site? You might make a brochure site extolling the features of your product. Will you get much attention? Probably not much.

Now let's say you're more imaginative like Artifice, the makers of DesignWorkshop, has been . Instead of just talking about their product, Artifice has made a fascinating site called Great Buildings (http://www.greatbuildings.com). The great buildings of the world are in a searchable database. Information is available on each building as well as photographs and 3D models of most of them. How do you view those models? Download a free copy of DesignWorkshop Lite. In addition, you can use it to design your own buildings. If you like it, Artifice hopes you'll upgrade to the Classic or Pro versions for a fee.

5 New Relationships

Hello, Harry Tennant. We have recommendations
for you in Books, Music, *and* more.

— Amazon.com

The second strategic theme that separates online business from offline
business is New Relationships. The Net enables and facilitates relationships between businesses and their customers, suppliers and
communities that are more difficult or even impossible offline.

The Net begins as a communication technology. It is not surprising
that it leads to changes in the way people communicate, which in
turn leads to changes in the type and character of relationships
among individuals and businesses on the Net. Many online companies are identifying each of millions of customers individually. They
come to know a great deal about these individuals, both through
conventional question and answer forms and through information
collected over time. The information may be collected through various forms on ongoing dialog and observing individual customers'
behavior. When this kind of information collection and exchange
happens among friends, it gives us a warm feeling of "getting to
know one another." When it goes awry, it generates a very different
feeling, an uncomfortable feeling of being spied upon or stalked.
There are significant benefits to both companies and their custom-

ers in using the online opportunity to build new relationships, which can be summarized by better service at lower cost.

A consequence of the New Relationships of the Net is a shift in the power among people and organizations through the Net. It appears that a current shift in the democratization of power we have seen on the Net is likely to be an enduring trend. Those who own printing presses or broadcast stations no longer control publication of editorial opinion to millions. Anyone with a Net connection can publish. If the message is compelling, it may spread to millions of readers literally overnight, at very little or no cost. Product sales occur within a context of a balance of power between buyers and sellers. Buyers generally gain power through aggregation and centralization, which is why governments work to control monopolies. But the Net tends to disaggregate and decentralize. There appears to be a power shift online in favor of buyers.

Many successful online businesses have developed strategies that embrace the New Relationships enabled by the Net. First, we will discuss some of the ways individual relationships are being built among organizations and their customers through getting to know customers individually, ongoing dialog and building communities. Then we will discuss the emerging power shift encouraged by the Internet in the web of companies and customers.

Individual Relationships

Relationship marketing (sometimes called one-to-one marketing) consists of several approaches:

- Differentiate products, service or marketing

- Differentiate individuals

- Build relationships over time

- Anticipate customer wants

- Direct customer contact

Differentiate products, service or marketing

The ultimate in differentiated products is the product customized to an individual. Similarly, service may be customized, as in special billing plans to suit individual customers. And each prospect may be approached in a different way. Customized products are offered through offline companies as well as online ones. However, doing business online makes some customized products very easy to produce and others easy to order.

The Design a Garden feature at Garden.com illustrates the link between customization and repeat business. Visitors to Garden.com are invited to use a Java applet to graphically lay out their gardens. They can then drag and drop plants into the layout. Similar applications are available on CDROMs but the problem is that after designing a garden with a CDROM application, it may be very difficult to find the plants. Garden.com's Design a Garden is tied directly to their inventory. Nothing appears that can't be bought. The gardener finishes the design, clicks a button and orders the plants.

The repeat business benefit comes from the fact that garden designs are saved on the site and can be called up later by the gardener. The gardener designs a garden in the spring and buys the
plants. She returns in the summer, modifies the garden for summer
plants and buys those. She returns again in the fall, pulls up the
design and so it goes. Customization and remembering help to
reinforce the relationship over time and help to keep customers coming back for more.

As discussed in the section on the New Economics of the Net, Texas
Instruments (http://www.ti.com), sends out over a hundred thousand weekly customized e-mail messages summarizing TI product
news for the previous week in the areas of interest specified by
individual customers. It's a way for TI to keep in contact with customers who have expressed an interest in TI products, but not to
bombard the customers with a lot of irrelevant and unwanted information about products that are not of interest.

Differentiate individuals

Individuals first must be identified, and then their behavior and preferences can be remembered and used as the basis for differentiated
products, service and marketing. Remembering individual differences and then customizing offerings is the essence of relationship
marketing.

One of the simplest ways to start building a personal relationship
with visitors and customers is to remember who they are and a little
about them. For example, the MovieLink (http://www.movielink.com)
site stores the visitor's name and zip code in a cookie and uses that

to display local theaters. It's a very simple idea, but it is a convenience for the visitors and helps MovieLink deliver the right information quickly.

One step up in complexity from a simple cookie as used by MovieLink
is a database of people with information about them—information
that makes it easy to buy.   Some obvious information to keep is
name, address and credit card information.   Amazon (http://
www.amazon.com) uses that well with their 1-Click Ordering buttons: once a customer is registered he need only click the 1-Click
Ordering button to have the book currently in view charged to his
credit card and sent to his address.

Another database notion, particularly appropriate for department
stores or malls, is the gift registry, such as the one available at the
J.C. Penney (http://www.jcpenney.com) site. An old idea brought
to the Web, it uses information about individuals to facilitate purchases.

Netmarket (http://www.netmarket.com) aims to provide nearly all
the products that consumers are likely to purchase. As a loyalty
incentive for their best customers, they offer Netmarket Cash, frequent shopper credits which can be applied to future purchases.
These credits are similar to airline frequent flier miles, which started
the era of computer-based relationship marketing. The airlines,
however, go much farther: the best individual customers (Gold and
Platinum members) have special ticket lines at the airport, early
boarding, free upgrades and other benefits to make them feel special.

Several florists (e.g., http://www.1800flowers.com), gift shops and greeting card companies (http://www.greetst.com) offer reminder services. The customer typically enters birthdays, anniversaries and selects from a list of holidays. He then receives e-mail reminders a few days before the event.

Most online grocery stores (e.g., http://www.netgrocer.com) facilitate frequent repeated purchases by maintaining a database of shopping lists for each customer. It's handy for the customer since he need only check off the familiar items he wants to buy. It's beneficial for the stores because the convenience of this individual's information keeps customers coming back.

Personalized Web pages have become popular on many sites. A typical example is My Yahoo (http://my.yahoo.com). Visitors can specify that their personal page should include news on selected topics, sports, weather for their area, current stock prices of interest, TV listings, movie listings, musical performances and other events of interest. The benefit to site visitors is that they get easy access to information of interest. The benefit to Yahoo? Personalized pages bring visitors back to the site more frequently and they tend to stay longer. Yahoo makes its money by selling advertising so these pages increase ad exposures and thus increase advertising revenues for Yahoo.

Build relationships over time

When a company identifies individuals and remembers their preferences and behavior, it implies a relationship over time. But it's not always clear how to maintain a relationship over time. And, in some cases, it may not make much sense, such as for products that are bought infrequently (houses, foundation repairs, wedding dresses) or that are too inexpensive to justify a relationship (candy, canned vegetables). But for those products where a relationship does make sense, how is it maintained effectively?

By far the most common approach to building and maintaining relationships over time are the techniques used periodically to bring the business to the customer's attention. Various forms of newsletters and discussions are used.

Periodic communication

When American Airlines (http://www.aa.com) designed their Web site, Net SAAver Fares was added almost as an afterthought, but it has become enormously successful. Visitors to the site can subscribe to the Net SAAvers service by selecting departure cities and arrival cities that interest them. They then receive weekly e-mails showing opportunities for discount travel to and from their selected cities. It's a good deal for American Airlines. The discounted seats typically travel within the next few days. American has an opportunity to sell seats that would otherwise likely fly empty, which would be a revenue opportunity forever lost. And it's a good deal for travelers. If one is ready to fly on short notice he can get a deeply discounted ticket.

Millions of Web site visitors have subscribed to Net SAAvers service. It cost American something to create the system, but it costs very little to run. The special fares between selected cities are simply a database query and the customized e-mail messages can be sent

across the Net for free.   Not only is this an example of the New
Economics of the Net, but it is also an example of the second strategic theme, the New Relationships available across the Net: American is in weekly contact with millions of potential customers at the
customer's request.

The Mountain Zone (http://www.mountainzone.com) is a highly successful Web site that has drawn millions of visitors in their couple of
years of operation.   But they consider e-mail to be their most successful marketing tool.   Every week they send a newsletter to more
than 90,000 subscribers, which results in a 15% increase in Web site
traffic.   To increase subscriptions to the newsletter, they offered a
free Everest screensaver, which increased subscriptions by 40%.

Cassette House (http://www.tape.com) sells recordable media—tapes,
recordable CDs, DATs—at great prices.   About 10% of the visitors to
the site buy something, so the trick is to bring in as many visitors as
possible.   Their chief means of doing so is their e-mail mailing list.
But we all get lots of those newsletters and never read them, right?
Cassette House keeps folks on the list and entices them to read by
offering incredibly good deals only to mailing list recipients.   In fact,
the deals are so good, they can only afford to offer them to a portion
of the list on each mailing.   They have virtually no attrition from the
mailing list.   Also, when customers come to the site for the special
private sales, 75% buy additional, regularly priced products.

Coastal Tool (http://www.coastaltool.com), probably the online market
leader in online sales of power tools, sends out a monthly newsletter
including category and tool reviews, new product introductions, pro-
motions and special pricing available only to newsletter subscribers.

Newsletter subscribers are likely a company's best customers. Coastal Tool is treating their best customers right: better information and better prices as a reward for their loyalty and continuing interest.

Communities

In addition to the Design a Garden feature, another type of relationship available through garden.com helps to build loyalty to the site. The online garden chat rooms are online counterparts to garden clubs, which have been popular for hundreds of years. If people have enjoyed discussing their gardens in their living rooms for that long, it makes sense that they would also enjoy discussing them online. And they do. Garden.com's (http://www.garden.com) online chat rooms are among the most popular parts of the Web site. Notice that, in this case, Garden.com is not building relationships between itself and site visitors, but enabling relationships among the site visitors themselves. Garden.com is simply offering the forum for the discussions. Nevertheless, from a business point of view, the effect is much the same. The gardeners who participate in the online discussions build relationships within their discussion groups and return to the Garden.com site to continue the discussions.

The Motley Fool site (http://www.motleyfool.com) provides information and analysis on investments; but the feature that is most active, and that which brings people back, is the community. The community is a collection of discussion groups to which visitors post about 5,000 messages each day. Visitors provide the content, the messages, which bring other visitors back for frequent visits. Motley Fool provides the venue where it can happen and along the way they sell ad space and a few products. The loyal visitors return for discussions with the rest of the community.

Discussions can increase the value of products. The calculator group at Texas Instruments (http://www.ti.com) sells scientific and educational calculators. On their Web site they offer discussion areas for customers interested in discussing the use of these calculators. Like the discussions at Garden.com, TI offers the forum for the discussions. However, the discussions increase the value of TI's calculator products. As customers talk to one another, they help each other write calculator programs and figure out how best to use the calculators in classrooms. The value of the product increases for everyone.

The Web site is an essential element in creating value for Esther Dyson's book, *Release 2.0*. She treats the book as if it were software. It's about online communities and the issues of life online. Like many books, there's an associated Web site (http://www.release2-0.com), but unlike most books, the Web site is integrated with the plan for the book. The site includes discussions. When the book first came out, a different chapter of the book was the featured discussion topic on the site each week. Now, anyone can comment on any topic anytime. The material from the discussions was incorporated into a book "update," called *Release 2.1*, released about a year later.

Auctions are part marketplace and part entertainment. Frequent auction participants form a community of sorts. We find an example of the business use of auction communities on the Net at Ancient Art - Online (http://www.AncientArt-Online.com). Selling ancient art is primarily a business of relationships. Buyers get to know dealers and get to trust them and their taste over time. Dealers build relationships with other dealers to find the kinds of pieces that their clients want.

The founder of Ancient Art - Online was a collector who simply wanted to sell some pieces through eBay. He was surprised at the high prices the eBay auctions generated and also by the number of contacts he made through participating in the auction. It was clear there was a business in this. Ancient Art - Online was born. They now have a Web site and offer pieces for sale. They still offer relatively inexpensive pieces (a few hundred dollars) for auction through eBay, not so much for the sales revenue, but to start new relationships with interested buyers. Typically, collectors spend increasing amounts on subsequent purchases with dealers, far more than would be spent in an eBay auction. The auction gets the relationship started.

A few years ago I read about a person who found just the car she wanted. Instead of buying it, she got on a newsgroup and rounded up ten others who wanted the same car, went to the dealer and they all got a deep discount for buying in quantity.

Mercata (http://www.mercata.com) turns that concept into a business. It brings together buyers across the Net for particular products and then buys for the group at a discount. They call it "We-commerce." It's another example of the Net's potential for shifting power from sellers to buyers.

Learning over time

Actually learning more about each customer over time can be more effective than simply getting the customer's attention periodically. The most common technique is collecting transaction information. The transaction information is then used to make particularly appealing offers to individuals based on what they have bought in the past. In the mail order business, which has tracked individual customers for decades, future buying is best predicted by RFM: recency, frequency and monetary. When did she last order, how frequently does she order, and how much does she spend?

Amazon and the other online booksellers collect information about individual customers and use that to offer special services. For example, they recommend books based on the books a customer has bought in the past and based on preferences she's disclosed. They let her look at her order history and the status of current orders. They let her order books with one click if she's revealed her name, address and credit card number.

Relationships come more naturally to some businesses than to others. Grocery sales are repeated at least once a week, so it makes sense to try to build information-based relationships around these frequent transactions. The frequent buyer cards now common in grocery stores will, when the data-handling techniques are in hand, give customers incentives to buy repeatedly at the same stores because the stores will know what each customer prefers. The stores will tailor their offerings to each customer's preferences. For example, a frequent buyer of Coca-Cola may get a great price on Coca-Cola. Another customer who prefers Pepsi gets a great price on that.

Computer sales are difficult to build a relationship on since they happen relatively infrequently. However, Gateway (http://www.gateway.com) has created a way of keeping the relationship active until it's time for the next computer purchase. Gateway's Your:)Ware program allows customers to lease computers with a "technology refresh" clause. Everyone knows that one of the problems in buying a computer is that it will soon be obsolete. The Your:)Ware program builds on that. Leasees can trade in their current Gateway computer after two years for a new one while, incidentally, extending their lease another two years. It's a clever way to encourage repeat sales while helping the customer deal with the problem of obsolescence. It's a way for Gateway to be a differentiated vendor when it's time for that next purchase. Gateway might even be viewed as moving from a product company to a service company. Instead of just selling computers (products), they are in the service of providing computing resources, even as computing technology changes.

Office Depot's online store (http://www.officedepot.com) offers the same idea but for office supplies. Not only does it help to keep the supply cabinet full, but Office Depot has a chance to know who its customers are and what they buy, which can be useful for future marketing. I have been shopping at a physical Office Depot store for years and they still have no idea who I am.

Nobody likes spam, unsolicited commercial e-mail. On the other hand, newsletters and product announcements sent by e-mail is one of the most cost-effective ways for companies and customers to communicate. The difference is that newsletters, when done properly, are *solicited* commercial e-mail. Even ads can be interesting and welcome if the recipient happens to be in the market for what is being advertised.

Opt-in e-mail advertising companies like Postmaster Direct build upon two ideas: the cost-effectiveness of e-mail advertising and the fact that when a potential buyer is interested in, say, tires, tire ads can be pretty darn fascinating!

Opt-in e-mail advertising collects e-mail addresses of buyers who want to receive ads in certain categories. These buyers have not just bought something else and unwittingly ended up on a mailing list, as is common in the offline direct marketing business. Rather, they asked to be sent e-mail ads. They are interested prospects. That's why e-mail ad campaigns to opt-in lists are uncommonly successful: typically 5-15% response rate.

Opt-in is based on three principles:

- Notice. Full disclosure of what data is being collected about the list member and how it will be used.

- Choice. Members must opt-in to join and may opt-out anytime they wish.

- Access. Members can check, modify or delete their records at any time.

Anticipate customer wants

Vendors see a lot of customers with similar needs, tastes and interests. They can use this experience to anticipate what may appeal to an individual customer.

BookMatcher is Amazon's (http://www.amazon.com) collaborative filtering function. BookMatcher works by collecting the likes and dislikes of many people on a collection of books. It then recommends new books to you by finding other people whose tastes match yours on books you've both read. It then looks for books the other people have read and ranked highly which you haven't read. BookMatcher then recommends those books to you.

We will revisit collaborative filtering later when discussing another Strategic Theme, Network Effects.

Direct customer contact

Companies that sell direct to their end customers have the advantage of learning from all the customers and can offer each customer products that more exactly fit her needs.

The online direct sales model of Dell Computer illustrates one of the most dramatic examples of the New Relationships of the Net. Dell was in an ideal position when e-commerce came along. First, they were already selling direct. They did not have conflict with existing channels of distribution, which has been a problem for many companies attempting to sell direct over the Net. Second, every computer that Dell sells is a custom computer. This is ideally matched to online sales because it is so easy to specify options through a Web page. Dell gains several advantages from its direct online sales. Since they have no finished product in distribution channels, they have no burden of unsold inventory. Also, since customers can specify exactly the options they want in a new computer, Dell gets immediate feedback on customer preferences with each order. And it all happens essentially in real-time.

Nike (http://www.nike.com) revolutionized the athletic shoe business by carefully designing shoes for particular purposes and differences in human anatomy. But all that design is for naught if the shoe salesperson cannot tell customers which shoe is designed for their needs. In a recent shoe-buying foray at a local shoe store, several types of shoes were recommended for me, not one of which was appropriate according to Nike. Part of the problem is selling indirect: the salespeople cannot keep up with the variety of shoes and needs. But a company that deals in the volumes that Nike deals in must rely, at least in part, on an indirect sales force. The problem is addressed in part by Nike's Product Recommendation system. The prospective customer answers around a dozen questions about himself and how he'll use the shoes and the Product Recommendation System reveals which shoes are right. The customer is thus armed to run into his local shoe store and ask for exactly what's right for him. Of course, it would be nice to just order the shoes through Nike's Web site, but their retail partners might not like that. (Unfortunately, on a recent visit to Nike's Web site I saw that the Product Recommendation System was gone. Too bad. I fear next time I try buying running shoes I'll be at the mercy of a salesperson who may have been hired just days before).

Most commerce Web sites collect information that facilitates future transactions. The information can also be used to make the product more convenient. For example, any airline will keep track of your frequent flier information. But if you book travel through BizTravel (http://www.biztravel.com), they keep track of all your frequent customer memberships, send pager alerts to all who need to know if a flight is delayed or canceled, send travel plans to designated recipients (assistants, significant others) and offer real time flight tracking. By aggregating transactions across many airlines, hotels, car rentals and other companies, BizTravel.com is able to serve a role much closer to consumer representative.

Let's assume that BizTravel becomes very popular. It would be making money by collecting transaction fees on the travel services it books. But at the same time, it would have collected a great deal of information about the travel habits and preferences of its customers, both individually and collectively. And it is information that cuts across many companies: multiple airlines, multiple car rental agencies and so on. Although those companies are much larger than BizTravel would likely be, BizTravel would have valuable customer-specific information that its partners could not gain on their own. That information is potentially much more valuable than the booking transaction fees.

Changing Business Relationships and Roles

Coordination

Low transaction costs across the Net encourage businesses to rethink the boundaries of their organizations. Retailers like Garden.com sell product without carrying inventory. Garden.com's reputation with customers hinges on the performance of suppliers. All of the suppliers must provide accurate inventory information, must handle order fulfillment in a consistent way and must handle returns and other customer service issues in a consistent way. The relationship between Garden.com and their suppliers must be very close to enable that degree of integration.

As mentioned in the chapter on New Economics, Cisco outsources most of the production of the routers it sells: 90% of the subassemblies, 55% of the final assembly. Frequently, Cisco takes an order for a router, passes it on to a contract manufacturer, who then builds it and ships it direct to the customer. Cisco never touches the final product.

The production quality of Cisco's routers is critical to their business, so Cisco engineers design the production methods that the production supplier will use. Furthermore, Cisco monitors the operations of suppliers in real time through Net connections. This way, Cisco enjoys the benefits of control and design responsibility for production but is not burdened with the capital cost of owning the factories. It allows them to be more nimble in a rapidly changing marketplace without losing touch with critical aspects of the business—a common risk with outsourced operations.

This style of very tightly integrated business between companies was previously seen almost exclusively within a single company. It demonstrates how low transaction costs enabled by the Net are changing the nature of relationships among companies.

Access

In the early days of the commercial Net, the notion of eliminating the middleman, disintermediation, was often mentioned as a great online agent of change. We've actually seen relatively little of this. Areas where we have seen disintermediation are where the intermediary extracted large profits by hoarding information or access. Some stockbrokers have suffered from the online trading companies such as eTrade (http://www.etrade.com) and Schwab (http://www.schwab.com). The online trading companies provide self-service access to stock trades. They offer lots of information from companies and analysts and they let individuals specify their own trades. Any stockbrokers who previously acted merely as order takers need to reconsider how they might add value. That role is no longer needed. Similarly, travel agents are getting squeezed as travel booking gets easier for consumers and business travelers to do themselves.

Despite early predictions, most product distributors have not been hurt by e-commerce. In fact, the first priority of many online retailers is to partner with a large distributor in order to offer the distributor's inventory through the online store.

Ingram Micro (http://www.ingrammicro.com) is the largest distributor of computer products, selling to 140,000 retailers. It was thought that the Net would jeopardize the business of distributors like Ingram Micro. If online stores could readily order from anyone, why not go direct to the manufacturer and cut out the expense of the distributor?

Another way to look at it is, what does a distributor like Ingram
Micro offer?

- Aggregate transactions. Retailers can get all kinds of computer products from many manufacturers by going to just
  one company.

- Breakdown quantity. Many manufacturers prefer to sell
  only in quantity. The distributor breaks large quantities
  down into smaller quantities.

- Communication. Distributors take on the role of communicating with retailers, perhaps in specialized markets.

- Financing. Distributors share some of the expense of getting products to market.

- Storage. Distributors offer less expensive storage space
  than most retailers have.

What gets easy and what stays hard as business moves to the Net?
The Net makes aggregating transactions easy. It makes communication easier, particularly finding customers and informing them about
products. Breaking down quantities is still a challenge. Storage still
has to happen (unless the products can be built on demand). Ingram
Micro is now breaking down quantities to quantities of one: They will
drop ship products directly to consumers. If someone drops out of
the distribution chain, perhaps it will be the bricks and mortar retailer rather than the distributor.

As the roles of some intermediaries seem to be changing, new ones are being created, zShops (http://www.amazon.com/zshops) being an example. First, there were lists of URLs of Web sites. Collected and categorized, they became Web directories, Yahoo! being the dominant example. Then there were word indices of Web pages, today exemplified by a handful of search engines such as AltaVista, Lycos, HotBot, Excite, Infoseek and Snap. A new generation of search facilities represents more of the meaning of the items they search for. zShops on Amazon's site indexes individual products for sale from specialty stores. Visitors can search for items across many specialty stores' Web sites, compare features and prices, and then click on the item they want to complete the sale. Amazon doesn't process or fulfill the orders. Amazon is merely an intermediary. They get paid by collecting affiliate rewards for referring customers to the vendors' sites.

Small consulting companies have difficulty locating the clients who need them. And the companies who need specialized consulting often have a hard time finding the consultants with the needed skills. Big consulting companies can afford to advertise since that cost can be amortized over a large number of consultants within the firm. Small consulting companies often can't afford to do that.

The Expert Marketplace (http://www.expert-market.com) is a new intermediary, a Web site that brings together consultants and the companies that need them. It lists 200,000 consulting firms, but the real business comes from the companies that have paid up to $2500/ year to join the Premier Expert Net group. They get prominent showing on searches for consultants. The Expert Marketplace makes money on the Premier Expert Net subscriptions as well as on commissions for leads that result in contracts.

Individuals have been unable to participate in initial public offerings (IPOs), which is often a very lucrative time to invest. When Wit Beer made their IPO, they did so through the Net, allowing individuals to get in on the investment opportunity. The IPO was a success. The founder of Wit Beer used that experience to create Wit Capital (http://www.witcapital.com), an online investment company that now helps other companies conduct their IPOs through the Net.

Wit also facilitates stock trading among members. In the Wit trading area, buyers and sellers locate one another directly and negotiate the trade. The middleman, the broker, is not necessary in this trading environment and so has been eliminated. By eliminating the broker, stock is traded without spreads (the difference between what the seller is asking and what the buyer is offering). The result is better deals for both buyers and sellers.

Priceline (http://www.priceline.com) is widely known online as a travel site offering reverse auctions: Customers name the price they are willing to pay for an airline ticket, for example, and Priceline looks for an airline willing to sell for that price. Priceline makes its money on the spread. If I bid (as I recently did) to buy a ticket from Dallas to Milwaukee for $450, which was about $75 less than any fare I could find by searching directly, Priceline finds the cheapest fare they can get, and then they sell it to me for $450. (Funny thing about these trades. When successful, it leaves me feeling like I must have bid too much). Priceline's reverse auction is an example of a more general notion of reverse markets.

Reverse markets are emerging everywhere on the Net these days, markets where sellers come to buyers rather than the other way around, the way it has traditionally been done. Monster.com (http://www.monster.com), one of the biggest job search Web sites, is creating a reverse market for people. Their Talent Market enables potential employers to bid on applicants.

No doubt Dilbert will have a field day with this concept and its similarity to human auctions of the past. Nevertheless, the Talent Market is another illustration of the shifting relationship between buyers and sellers brought about by online marketplaces.

6 New Timing

OK, so let's say you find something on eBay that you really want.... You're willing to pay $25.00 for it, but the current bid price is only $2.25. You could take the long route and sit at your computer, outbidding each new bid until you reach $25.00. (Like you have nothing better to do...!)

Luckily, there's a better way: Let the system be your proxy and do your bidding for you.

— Proxy bidding, eBay.com

Business moves faster on the Net. It's known as *Internet time*. It seems that the perception of Internet time started with Netscape. Business on the Internet began with the graphical Web browser, the first example of which was the Mosaic browser developed at the University of Illinois. It was made available over the Net for free. It was extremely popular. It was quickly downloaded and installed by users around the world. The developers soon left the university to form Netscape, which offered an improved browser. It too was made available for free over the Net and was promptly downloaded and installed by people all over the world. Netscape came out with new generations of browser software every few months. Because it was so easy and free to download and install each generation, users very quickly replaced the preceding generations. Then Microsoft got into the browser business and started offering versions of its Internet Explorer browser for free as well. The versions were released a few months apart instead of a few years apart, which is more typical for software. In the meantime, Netscape went public within nine months of its founding and racked up what was to be one of the first of many unprecedented valuations of Internet companies. It seemed everything was moving uncommonly fast—changing on Internet time.

Two of the main drivers of Internet time are the other strategic themes we've already considered: the New Economics of the Net and the New Relationships of the Net. The New Economics of the Net makes it possible to distribute information and products at little or no cost, which eliminates one of the primary barriers to adoption of new products. The New Relationships of the Net make it much easier to connect to customers and make it much easier for competitors to evaluate what the competition is doing, then generate a rapid response. This acceleration of product distribution, acceptance, building brand awareness and competitive response is becoming characteristic of online business. The New Timing of the Net.

The New Timing of the Net applies to other sorts of tasks as well. Many tasks can be completed much more rapidly simply because information is readily accessible over the Net. For example, books can be located and ordered in less time that it would take to back the car out of the garage if one were going to drive to a local bookstore to buy the book. And when you drive to the store, will the book be in stock?

A client recently told me that when they release a new consumer product, they get many thousands of the "warranty reply" cards back, typically a 5% return rate. First, they said that marketing doesn't record the information due to data entry costs. Then they admitted that marketing only looks at the first 10,000 cards to get a general "impression" of the customers. When probed, they confessed that maybe it was more like 500. And marketing might not get around to looking at the cards for months after the product launch. Finally, the "warranty cards" were not required for the warranty at all.

My suggestion: Do product registration through the Web as many software companies such as Microsoft already do. Data entry costs drop to zero. The data is available for immediate statistical analysis, not just "general impressions." The data is available instantly. The questionnaire can even be modified as early returns raise new questions.

The response rate may drop some, but it would still be better than getting 5% returns but throwing most of them away unseen. Better yet, provide an incentive to online registration such as some software or an applications booklet. This might generate a much higher rate of registration. Best of all, with online product registration, the company can identify their customers and can continue to serve and learn from them into the future.

The American Airlines Net SAAvers fare service, described in the section on New Relationships is also an example of the New Timing of the Net. The idea of offering discounted fares for airline seats that are about to fly empty is not new. However, the Net offers a great advantage in timing. Discounted fares can be offered for last minute sale and can be announced to millions of people who have already indicated their interest. The New Timing of the Net allows things to happen on a shorter time scale, creating opportunities that were previously impractical.

Locating an address on a street map anywhere in the country through sites like maps.yahoo.com can now be done more quickly than was possible offline. On a recent trip to San Francisco, I had the address of the company I needed to visit in the city. My only purpose for the trip was that early morning meeting, so I located the company on a map at Yahoo!Maps (http://maps.yahoo.com), then requested a list of hotels, ordered by distance from the meeting. There was a convention in town, so all the national brand hotels were sold out. The sort-by-distance list of hotels made finding a good nearby local hotel quick and easy.

A lot of common tasks get much quicker and easier because the information is readily available on the Net. Take comparison-shopping, for example. I recently needed to buy a minidisc recorder. A search for "minidisc" on Yahoo!Shopping (http://shopping.yahoo.com) returned 308 products from 58 stores as well as a review of minidisc recorders. With a few clicks I saw the differences among the available models. Once I had identified the model that best suited my needs, another search for that model number gave me a list of about a dozen stores that offered it. I chose the one with the best price. The entire process took about an hour. In contrast, it takes me twenty minutes to drive over to my local Best Buy and they have only two models to choose from. Yes, I had to wait for delivery (it arrived the next day), but that's a tradeoff I'll gladly make. It's not time that takes my attention, which is the time that is most valuable to me. Another aspect of the New Timing of the Net.

Time that takes attention suggests another aspect of the New Timing of the Net. The technical contribution of the Net is that it offers faster and cheaper transactions. It's not just faster and cheaper communication; telephones and fax machines do that, too. But the Net, with computers at every node, connects the communication links with the ability to process and act on the information flowing through them. Those are transactions, whether they are familiar business transactions or simply forwarding or accepting and acknowledging an e-mail message. As the Net makes transactions cheaper and faster, entire categories of human activities can get cheaper and faster, too.

Consider, for example, proxy bidding in auctions at eBay.com. When you bid for an item at eBay, someone else may outbid you. You can keep rechecking the status of the auction (requiring your time and attention) or you can enable proxy bidding. With proxy bidding, you specify how high you're willing to let your bid go and by what increments you'll outbid a rival. If you are outbid, your proxy bidder will automatically increase your bid by your specified increment until either no one outbids you or you reach your specified maximum bid. So you either get the item you want at the lowest possible bid or you let it go to someone who wants it more than you, but the process has taken a minimum of your time and attention. The New Timing of the Net.

DealTime (http://www.dealtime.com) is an online comparison shopping service with a twist. While most price comparison services link to a collection of stores, DealTime adds links to auctions and classified ads. Shoppers can either select an item to purchase through the DealTime site or can set up a bot to watch for a specific product at a given price. In addition, DealTime offers several ways to notify users of the deals they've found: pager, e-mail or the Desktop Notifier. The Desktop Notifier is software for a desktop or palmtop computer that flashes notification when DealTime has found the deal that the user has been waiting for.

DealTime makes its money through advertising on the site and merchant fees. Their Desktop Notifier offers a targeted advertising opportunity when the user has already expressed an interest to buy.

Spam, unsolicited commercial e-mail, is a bad problem that appears to be getting worse. Where there's a problem, there's an opportunity. Bright Light has created a way to detect and block spam, nearly in real time.

Bright Light (http://www.brightlight.com) has deployed a network of probe e-mail accounts distributed across the Net. These accounts are bait for spammers. When one receives e-mail, an alert is sent to the Bright Light Operations Center where people (not programs) examine the incoming unsolicited e-mail and determine whether it qualifies as spam. If it does, "spam wall" (analogous to firewall) software located at ISPs is notified of the offending messages, which are then deflected into a special folder of suspect messages. All other messages are passed through to the ISP's customers' normal e-mail.

The system works because it takes some time to send out a large volume of e-mail. The probe accounts detect the first wave of a spam campaign, then the system responds rapidly enough to block the offending messages for most other users on the Net.

The benefits of faster transactions are amplified when applied to business-to-business transactions. A priority at Dell Computer is to wring time out of their processes. The time that parts sit in inventory, for example, not only ties up Dell's cash; but, in the fast-moving computer business, parts in inventory are constantly losing value, constantly moving toward obsolescence. The same holds true for inventory of finished goods. If finished computers sit in inventory in a warehouse or retail store, they are tying up cash and continuously losing value. Dell addresses the problem of finished goods inventory by not having any—by selling direct and building each computer to order. They address the problem of parts inventory by replacing inventory with information. Parts suppliers are electronically linked to Dell. As soon as Dell receives an order for a computer, news is passed on to the parts suppliers for that computer. This way, suppliers know in real-time how quickly Dell is using their parts and can adjust their production accordingly. By eliminating time delays, Dell and its suppliers can eliminate inefficiencies in the supply chain. The New Timing of the Net.

Dell's direct sales model and speed of execution has created a very favorable situation for them: They can grow quickly without a cash flow problem.

Growth is expensive. It's so expensive, in fact, that seemingly successful companies sometimes flounder from too much growth. If a company is growing quickly, it typically requires a lot of cash to make products that are then distributed to retail outlets and eventually sold. From the time the parts are ordered until the time they are sold, they are tying up cash. The faster the growth, the more cash is tied up in parts and finished goods. But parts for next month's higher revenues must be paid for with the cash from last month's lower revenues. Sometimes fast growth companies run out of cash.

Dell has found a way to let its customers fund its growth without a cash crisis. When Dell takes a credit card order for a custom computer, the credit card funds are usually available within 24 hours. The computer is built and shipped typically within five days, so they have the money in hand while the computer is being built. Furthermore, they have just-in-time inventory arrangements with their parts suppliers. Dell takes possession of parts at almost the same time that the computer is being built, then pays for the parts within 15 days—with funds they already have from the credit card purchase. So customers' credit cards fund Dell's growth. It works because of speed: There is no delay between customer orders and Dell's knowledge of them, the just-in-time inventory system works off of real time information, and Dell's build-to-order production is so fast that charging the customers' credit cards on the order day rather than on the ship day is inconsequential to the customers (who won't get the credit card bill for a month, anyhow.)

Motorcyle Online (http://www.motorcycle.com) is a Net magazine that's been profitable since 1995—longer than most other sites have been online. They've identified a few keys to their success.

- Their reviews of motorcycles are not influenced by the potential impact of a negative review on ad revenue. If the product is lousy, they say it's lousy.

- Motorcycle Online can be far more responsive than a print publication. They can get an article or review online within days, not months like a print publication.

- Motorcyle Online pays close attention to the logs: They know which articles are being read and which are not, and that's what guides editorial decisions.

We might summarize Motorcycle World's key to success as, "Serve the reader," the rest will follow. In serving the reader, their competitive advantage over print publications is time and its action counterpart, responsiveness.

Another example of real time relationships over the Net is illustrated by the Altrade system from Altra Energy (http://www.altra.com). The Altrade system is an Internet exchange that brings together buyers and sellers to trade in energy products: electricity, natural gas, crude oil and liquids. Traders are presented with a screen that looks essentially like a spreadsheet. That display connects back to a trading system through the Internet. With a couple of clicks of a mouse a trader can bid for and buy products in real time as they are offered by other traders through the Altrade system. At any time approximately 1,500 to 2,000 buyers and sellers are accessing the Altrade exchange. In the past, sellers made their energy products available through phone calls and faxes to thirty or forty people, which took time. With the Altrade system, as soon as a product is posted, hundreds of traders see it immediately. When a deal is struck, it happens virtually instantaneously. Traders can execute two to four times the number of trades in an hour than they were able to do previously.

Markets are as old has civilization itself. The benefit that Altrade provides is access to this specialized business-to-business market-place from anywhere in the world at any time. Not only is the rate of exchange accelerated (New Timing), but since the exchange is on the Web, many more traders can have ready access and they can get to the exchange from anywhere, which leads to the next strategic theme: Dissolution of Distance.

7 Dissolution of Distance

Outpost.com erbjuder ett fantastiskt urval av hårdvara, programvara och tillbehör för datorer. Vi har flera års erfarenhet av leverans av våra produkter över hela världen och ett globalt anseende för vår utmärkta internationella kundservice. Våra 160 000 datorprodukter från ledande tillverkare innefattar persondatorer, laptopdatorer, handdatorer, skrivare, bildskärmar, modem, acceleratorer, digitala kameror, DVD-enheter, förbrukningsartiklar, böcker med mera. Om det har att göra med datorer kan du vara ganska säker på att vi har det.

— Outpost.com, introduction in Swedish,
one of 13 languages supported by the site

On the Internet distance means nothing. When you access a Web site from your desktop computer, it doesn't matter whether that site resides on a server in your town, across the country or around the world. Distance just means nothing. The pages of the sites will be delivered to you at a speed that's determined by the speed of the server and the speed of your connection to the Net, but in most cases not by the distance between your computer and the server. This has important implications for business on the Net.

There are about 1000 mega-bookstores in the United States. About two-thirds of them are Barnes & Noble bookstores and most of the rest are Borders bookstores. In my neighborhood in North Dallas, for example, there are two Barnes & Noble bookstores and two Borders bookstores. Why so many? These mega-bookstores are primarily differentiated by location.

Amazon.com was the first mega-bookstore on the Internet. Several others soon followed: first, Barnes & Noble, next Borders and then others. In five years, how many mega-bookstores will there be on the Net? Will there be 1000? I don't think so. A hundred? I would guess a handful, maybe three to five. There will probably be lots of specialty bookstores, but only a small number of the very large bookstores that offer essentially every book in print. Why? Because of the Dissolution of Distance. On the Net distance means nothing, so the location means nothing, so every mega-bookstore is in virtually the same place. The scramble among businesses on the Net today is in part due to this realization. Several online markets already have established leaders. Amazon.com is the leader in books. eBay.com is the leader in consumer auctions. Yahoo! is the leader in Web site directory search and other reference material.

Once the customers and marketplace have decided who the market leader is, that leader becomes difficult to dislodge. It would not be easy for a rival to overtake Amazon's position as the leading online mega-bookstore. However, many online markets have not yet settled on a market leader. Opportunities are still open. Businesses are rushing to the Net in the hope of gaining market leadership when it is easiest to do so, as the online markets emerge. Market leadership opportunities will quickly disappear as customers choose the companies they wish to do business with in each marketplace. In a few years most of the market leaders will have been established.

The Net has already started changing the way business is done at a distance. In the past, trade over great distances meant trade in physical goods, whether it was salt in Roman times, silk a millennium later, or jet aircraft a millennium after that. But the Net is changing this. The economics of providing services at great distances is becoming much more attractive.

Jones International University (http://www.jonesinternational.edu) became the first accredited online-only university in 1999. It joined many other universities that offer degree programs online, such as the first to do so, the University of Phoenix. And there are hundreds of universities that offer distance learning courses, if not degrees, over the Net. Distance learning illustrates the potential of the Net to offer services, not just goods, to anyone anywhere.

The Net is good at moving information. Among its greatest successes is discussions. What is a university if not an environment for moving information around and the discussion of the ideas contained in those bits? Those bits can be moved without the expense of physical buildings for the schools and the expense of being physically present for the students. Education is an area where the Net may bring significant cost reductions.

What about quality? Did you ever sleep through a college lecture? It's no longer an excuse when lectures and other course materials are available on demand online. Certain courses present a problem: the equipment needed for chemistry labs, for example. But for most courses, there is great promise in putting education online.

Another aspect of education is the interaction with others taking the course. Can students find the same degree of interaction in online courses as offline courses? Many students, especially working students pursuing MBAs and other post-graduate work, find that there is actually more interaction among students in online courses. It is built into the curriculum. And since online discussions are not real time, they can be done when it is convenient to each participant. In fact, instructors often complain that online courses require a significantly larger time commitment because of the additional interaction time.

ZD University (http://www.zdu.com) offers over 150 instructor-led classes and a couple dozen more self-paced courses. In the instructor-led classes, students receive a reading assignment each week from the instructor. They can then ask questions and discuss the material with other students through threaded discussion groups in the virtual classroom. In addition to the classroom, each course also has a Class Cafe where students can post messages to one another about topics other than those covered in the class. Yet another discussion area, The Lounge, allows students to congregate with students from other ZD University classes.

Another aspect of ZD University contributes to community building. Membership in the university is paid for with a flat monthly fee. A registered student can take as many courses as he likes if there's room available. As a result, students have an opportunity to get to know one another over time and in more than one class.

In 1992 all-electronic brokerages appeared on America Online and Compuserve. In 1996, with the launch of E*Trade's Web site (http://www.etrade.com), demand for discount online brokerage services began to explode. By early 1999, more than a third of all retail trades were conducted online, and the shift to online trading continues.

E*Trade, Charles Schwab and the other online stock trading companies, are providing service at a distance. Investors from nearly every country in the world buy and sell stocks through the Web sites of these companies. Services are customized to reflect individual customers' interests, including portfolio tracking, real time stock quotes, market news, research, as well as trading. It is available anytime from anywhere around the world.

Collaboration used to mean that the collaborators worked in the same place. As telecommunication improves, collaboration at a distance gets easier. Eventually, collaboration at a distance will likely be no more difficult than e-mail at a distance. The Search for Extra-terrestrial Intelligence (SETI) is looking for the signatures of radio communication elsewhere in the cosmos. It involves a huge amount of signal processing of radio telescope data. In fact, it requires more processing power than is available to those doing the searching. But there is a great wealth of unused computer cycles in the world.

Most computers waste their time in idle loops most of the time. The Net can put the need together with the available computer cycles, in spite of the fact that the computers may be located anywhere on the planet.

SETI@Home is a program whereby anyone connected to the Net can download some software, run a small piece of the signal-processing problem, and then send the results back across the Net. At the time of this writing, about 184,000 computers were crunching away on SETI data and had already racked up over 216 *years* of CPU time.

I often get calls from charitable organizations for donations of clothing, used furniture and the like. When will charities solicit CPU cycle donations over the Net? When will I be able to deduct donated cycles from my taxes?

The Net is enabling people to work together more effectively at a distance. WebEx (http://www.webex.com) from ActiveTouch is a way to conduct meetings with a dispersed group. Meeting participants can talk over the phone while WebEx connects them and coordinates presentations. The meeting leader can synchronize PowerPoint presentations or software demos on the computers of all the meeting participants while explaining over the phone what they're seeing on the computer screen. Up to 25 participants can be added to a meeting. Meetings are mediated through WebEx for a fee.

Another corollary to the Dissolution of Distance is that promotion is more important on the Net than in the physical world. Why? In the physical world, location is important because it's a primary form of promotion: people know about your store because they see it right there on that busy corner or in the bustling mall. Promotion based on presence doesn't work on the Net in the midst of 400,000,000 other Web pages. The online entrepreneur must make up for this with more strenuous promotional efforts. It can be done, but don't imagine that setting up shop online implies that you'll start to get business.

When we announce new Web sites, many tend to be too local in their thinking. Should you, for example, announce your site in Australia, even if there is no specific Australian content in it? A candidate site is Alan Farrelly's Net News site (http://technology.news.com.au/netnews) that features Internet news, updated daily. But this is the Net where distance means nothing. Here are two facts to consider: 60% of the readership of Net News is from the U.S. and visitors from Australia or anywhere else in the world with decent connectivity can get to your site about as easily as another visitor living right next door. The question is not, where are they? The question is, who are they and would they be interested in my site?

Yet another corollary of the Dissolution of Distance is that any business on the Net is potentially a global business. The Cyberian Outpost was a small computer store in a strip mall in the small town of Kent, Connecticut. They used to get about a half-dozen walk-in customers per day. Then they put their store online. They took the global opportunity of the online business seriously, offering their site in any of eleven languages. The online store is now called Outpost.com (http://www.outpost.com) and is one of the leading online computer retailers. The number of "surf-in" customers per day are now counted in the tens of thousands. It underscores the opportunity of the Dissolution of Distance. The entire population of Kent, Connecticut is only 3,500!

Global business implies dealing with many languages, many currencies and a tangle of tax laws. But the business issues go beyond that. In Japan, for example, products purchased on the Net are generally not shipped to the buyer's home. Over 90% of Japanese are within a five-minute walk or drive of a convenience store, which are open 24 hours. Rather than have products shipped to their homes, Japanese online purchases are shipped to a local convenience store and picked up at the buyer's convenience. Furthermore, credit card use is relatively low in Japan. Payment is typically made with cash or check at the convenience store. The Dissolution of Distance offers the possibility of global business, but actually growing a global business may be something entirely different.

8 Network Effects

Get Your Private, Free E-mail at http://
www.hotmail.com
— Hotmail message tag line

America Online is in the business of delivering
subscribers to one another.
— Steve Case, CEO, AOL

Bob Metcalfe, inventor of Ethernet, first described what has become known as Metcalfe's Law.

The value of the network increases with the square of the number of users.

Consider the value of the telephone. One telephone is worthless. There is no one to call. When two people have telephones, each can call the other. When three people have telephones each can call any of the others. And so it goes. The more people who have telephones, the more valuable each telephone becomes. That is a Network Effect, Metcalfe's Law in action.

Steve Case, CEO of America Online, has said that AOL is in the business of delivering subscribers to one another. AOL offers lots of information resources but the main value to subscribers is that they can send and receive e-mail, join chat groups, see how others vote on polls and so on. AOL's business is to create a Network Effect among its subscribers.

At Amazon.com each page that describes a book has a section called "Customers who bought this book also bought:." It has another section called "Customer comments." Amazon shoppers benefit from the Network Effect of other Amazon shoppers.

Firefly pioneered the idea of collaborative filtering: collecting preferences on, say, movies, comparing your preferences with others and using that to suggest things (movies) you'd probably like but haven't seen yet. The technique works well for finite collections of things (movies, CDs, software, etc.). It is an example of a Network Effect. The more people's preferences are recorded in the system, the more valuable the system can be for all users.

Most applications of collaborative filtering work off a database of collected preferences—what people say they like. Ultramatch, from the search site Infoseek, puts a new twist on this idea. Ultraseek collects behavioral data on users: the terms they search for and the ads they click on. This is compared with other users and Ultramatch displays ads that a user's past behavior suggests he's likely to be interested in, i.e., likely to click on.

One of the most dramatic Network Effects is known as viral marketing. Anyone who has been online for a while has received jokes in their e-mail. And if they're funny, they are likely to be forwarded to several friends. Jokes travel through the Net at an amazing speed. One person forwards it to several others, many of whom forward it

to several others, and so it goes. A good joke travels to an expo-
nentially growing audience and spreads as quickly as people read
their e-mail. A good joke spreads like a highly contagious virus.
Viral marketing works the same way.

Hotmail was one of the early successes of viral marketing. Hotmail
offers users free e-mail and makes money through advertising. The
viral aspect of the business is in one line attached to the bottom of
each message that users send: "Get Your Private, Free E-mail at
http://www.hotmail.com." With that line, everyone who receives an
e-mail from a Hotmail member is exposed to Hotmail promotion. So
the Hotmail members are the ones doing the advertising. In addition, there's an implied endorsement of Hotmail from an acquain-
tance. After all, the one sending the message is a Hotmail member
and the recipient is probably someone he knows.

This approach was remarkably successful. Hotmail signed up more
than a million subscribers in its first six months of operation, spend-
ing only $50,000 on promotion. In the following months, Hotmail
signed up over ten million subscribers before being acquired by
Microsoft, 18 months after it opened for business. The subscription
base continues to grow quickly.

In order to get a Hotmail account, one need only fill out a questionnaire of demographic information. The demographic information is
then used for targeted advertising to the Hotmail subscribers. So
not only did Hotmail build a list of over a million names in six months,
but each of those names came complete with demographic information and an agreement to receive advertising.

Software can also be viral. One of the problems of software sales is that once one person has the software, he can give his friends copies who can give their friends copies and so on. Of course, it violates copyright laws, but the practice is not uncommon.

One can think of this sort of software piracy as a viral marketing opportunity. Release Software (http://www.releasesoft.com) has developed an e-commerce application that can be embedded in other software packages. It enables try-before-buy use of the software on a limited basis, and then requires that the user purchase the software to continue using it. Instead of fighting software sharing, Release has joined with the practice and helped make it a viable business.

Metcalfe's Law applies to programming languages also. One of the main reasons that Perl is a valuable language is that lots of other people use it. Each additional Perl programmer adds a little value to all the rest because a culture of giving away code has grown up around Perl (partly because it's difficult to hide your source code in this language.) This network of users creates reusable code (available at http://www.cpan.org) and creates a demand for Perl to be available on every server. Its ubiquity encourages more programmers to use it, which reinforces demand for its availability. More programmers means more available software and on it goes.

Steve Jurvetson, Managing Director at Draper Fisher Jurvetson, the venture capital firm that backed Hotmail, describes what he calls the Four Laws of Viral Marketing.

- That's what friends are for.

The great thing about viral marketing is that friends like to tell their friends about products and services that excite them. The idea of viral marketing is to base business promotion on that concept. The Net offers a collection of new ways for people to talk to one another. We saw examples in the section on the New Relationships of Net. Your business may enable communication through e-mail, through discussion groups, through affiliate programs or through telling book customers what other books people buy who have bought the book you're currently looking at. The important point is to make it possible for people to tell their friends about your products.

The electronic greeting cards at eGreetings (http://www.egreetings.com) are free. The site is supported by advertising. eGreetings helps to promote its site very simply with each card that's sent. Each card recipient can be thought of as a new customer. Whenever someone is sent a card from eGreetings, he or she is invited to send another card back for free. It's a simple way for eGreetings to build on the connections between its customers to build traffic.

Anyone can build gizmoz on the Zapa site (http://www.zapa.com). Gizmoz are customized applets such as photo albums, ID cards, greeting cards and animated buttons. The applets are free and cute— cute enough for people to want to send them (or pointers to them) to their friends and relatives. The benefit to Zapa: a marketing message can go along with them. Promotion by customers.

- The freer it is, the faster it spreads.

Cost is typically one of the biggest barriers to adopting new products or services. The lower the cost, the more ready people are to try new things. This is one of the opportunities that the Net provides, especially for information products services. We saw examples in the section on the New Economics of the Net. New browsers may be adopted quickly when they are made available for free. Of course, money needs to be made somewhere. Netscape benefited from a paired product strategy between its secure browser and its secure server. The browsers were given away for free, which increased the demand for Netscape's secure servers. Id Software used "drug dealer marketing." It gave away the level 1 version of Doom, creating demand for level 2 and level 3 from those addicted to the experience of playing level 1. The strategy at Hotmail was to provide free e-mail service in trade for demographic information and advertising exposures. The basic version of the popular e-mail software package Eudora is distributed for free. Upgrades to more capable versions are sold for a fee. Some products are offered for free initially, and then sold after they become widely used. Netscape tried this for a while, but since Microsoft continued to give away its browser for free, Netscape was forced to stop charging. The operating system Linux is available for free, but companies charge for support and consulting. The ESPN sports site offers a great deal of information for free but also offers additional information and commentary only to subscribers.

Online services generate revenues through a relatively small number of mechanisms. Most use advertising, sponsorship, subscription, referrals, service fees or transactions. Commercial sites need to make money through one of these mechanisms sooner or later, but the longer that free services can be provided to people on the Net, the more likely it is that the service will become widely known and widely used.

- Cafes beat subway stations.

People like lingering in cafes over a cup of coffee, a snack and conversation with their friends. On the other hand, lots of people pass through subway stations but they rarely stop to converse. Companies building their presence on the Net are better off creating a space where people enjoy their contact with other people. It's an atmosphere conducive to spreading the word about your products services. Discussion areas, opportunities to vote on an issue, online games, real time chat with friends all are examples of online spaces that foster interaction among people.

ICQ (I seek you—get it?) is an instant message system that works across the Net. When a circle of friends have each downloaded the ICQ software (http://www.icq.com), they can find out whether others in the circle are currently online and can send them instant messages.

One might set up an ICQ circle with just one other person, but it is more common for larger groups to form. Each member encourages several others to sign up. While gift giving may help spread the word about a service to one more prospect at a time, this is viral marketing with a high branching factor—each customer encourages many others to join. The higher the branching factor, the faster the growth.

- Size does matter.

One of the most powerful competitive barriers on the Net is market leadership. In many cases, the biggest businesses are the most likely to survive. If that's true, then building a large subscriber base quickly is one of the most important tasks that a new online business has.

How impressed should you be with a company that's been around since 1995, still hasn't made a profit, and recently lost $16 million on revenues of $65 million? What if that company also had 50 million registered users? And what if that company's product is a network product so it benefits from the Network Effect: the more people who use it, the more valuable it is for all users? And what if that company serves multimedia needs over the Net, the use of which will explode soon as more Net users get higher bandwidth connections?

Real.com (http://www.real.com), the makers of well-known brands, RealAudio and RealVideo, is one of the high-flying Internet stocks in spite of losses. It appears, however, that their strategy makes sense. The strategy: Build brand recognition and get their multimedia platforms installed everywhere despite losses. The only cloud in their future is whether Microsoft will be able to replace the RealNetworks multimedia platform on tens of millions of PCs with a Microsoft version.

Netscape (http://www.netscape.com) has ridden the exponential growth curve of Metcalfe's Law of network value. First, they had to displace the popular Mosaic browser. Netscape created a platform for secure transactions. They gave away the browser but sold the servers which, when connected to Netscape browsers, enabled encrypted transactions. Each Nescape browser helped increase demand for Netscape servers and vice versa.

But then Netscape derived value from a surprising source: Those free browsers had the Netscape Web site installed as the default browser home page. People tend not to change defaults, so this generated a huge amount of traffic to Netscape. Today their site is an advertising-based, revenue-generating portal.

Part III
Differentiation Strategies: How to Make a Net Business Unique

GE will be number one or number two in every market.

If you don't have a competitive advantage, don't compete.

— Jack Welch, CEO, GE
Called by *Business Week*,
"America's #1 Manager"

Markets are defined in the minds of customers. When a person thinks of a familiar product category, she typically thinks of one or two or three companies that fill that category. If pressed, she may be able to come up with a much longer list, but only if pressed. When I think of soft drinks, for example, I think of Coke and Dr Pepper. I am fully aware that there are many others, but I typically choose one of those two.

The market leader is the company that comes to mind most often with the most customers when it's time to buy. Because of its place in the minds of customers, the market leader makes more sales with less effort which means more profit. It's good to be the market leader.

When a business addresses a market that already has a leader, it has two options:

- displace the current market leader in the minds of customers or

- define a new market in the minds of customers and become the leader in that.

Both approaches have their challenges; but whichever approach is taken, the business must differentiate its offering from those already out there. The business must either convince customers that their offering is different and better than the current market leader or that it is so different it deserves a category of its own in customers' minds. This is the differentiating strategy.

Differentiation has two important components. First, the difference must make a difference to the customers—a difference they're willing to pay for. I see commercials on TV telling me that one brand of gasoline has additives that no other brand has. I don't care. They wasted their ad dollars on me because that difference makes no difference to me. On the other hand, when considering buying a digital camera, one stored images on cheap and abundant floppy disks while others used expensive solid-state memories. That difference was important to me and was the deciding issue in my purchase decision. That difference made a difference to me. On the Net, there are two main kinds of search: directories of sites like Yahoo! and indices of Web pages like Lycos. It's a difference that makes a difference. However, the differences between the page indices like Lycos, Hotbot, Excite and Dogpile don't make a difference to me.

The second component of differentiation is that the difference should be sustainable. A difference is sustainable only if competitors cannot readily copy it and thereby erase the difference. Patents are designed to make innovations sustainable differences. Exclusivity agreements are designed to make alliances sustainable differences. Economies of scale often make market share differences sustainable. Success with an existing business model can make the market leader reluctant to change, which means that a differentiating business model could be a sustainable difference. However, no differentiation strategy will create sustainable differences in all circumstances. Also, even sustainable differences can be copied in time. Sustainable differences should always be thought of as temporary, but more sustainable is better than less sustainable. Yahoo!Broadcast has signed many exclusive online broadcast agreements with radio stations, businesses, sports broadcasters, universities and others, which has created a sustainable difference.

Once a business has chosen its differentiating strategy, it takes la-
ser-like focus on that one difference to make the difference clear to
all the employees and more important, to make it clear to the customers. It's the one thing the company should concentrate on above
all others. It's the difference that will make a difference.

The following chapter discusses generic strategies for attaining market leadership. Then we will discuss several approaches to differentiation strategy, followed by consideration of how to choose the best
strategy. Finallywe will discuss aspects of the problem of reserving
a place for your business in the minds of your customers: brand
building.

9 Leadership Strategies

I think if you can combine first mover advantage with speed, it's very important. In other words, if you can get out into the marketplace as we did and early on capitalize on that first mover advantage to have millions of members before anyone else wakes up to what you're doing, that can be a huge advantage. I think if you're a first mover and you're slow...it doesn't mean much at all.

— Steve Markowitz
CEO, MyPoints.com

First Mover Advantage

Amazon.com was not the first online bookstore, but it was the first to be broadly recognized. And it was the first online mega-bookstore, offering millions of titles. It became first in the minds of online shoppers. Its current revenues are about 10 times that of its closest online rival, BarnesandNoble.com. Why? Does it carry more books? No. Are the books cheaper? No. Are they different books? No. Amazon.com became first in the minds of online book shoppers; and if they continue to innovate, they have the opportunity to keep that position for years to come. The great thing about being the leader: it's typically much more profitable. Advertising dollars have a bigger impact, customers tend to give leaders the benefit of the doubt, and they are often willing to pay a premium price for the leader's products.

Hoping to do for greeting cards what Amazon did for books, Sparks.com (http://www.sparks.com/) offers far more paper cards (over 13,000 as of February, 2000) than offline stores, which typically stock a few hundred cards. They bill themselves as The World's Largest Greeting Card Store. They offer all relationship features that make sense for a greeting card company: reminder e-mails, a personal address book and a calendar. They will send the cards for their customers or send them to the customer for her to send out.

Sparks.com was started with the idea that cards are mostly bought by women (average 30/year vs. 4/year by men) and that working women have difficulty getting to stores to buy cards. Online shopping can help the women and maybe the reminder service will even help the men!

Unlike offline greeting cards stores, online stores are not differentiated by location. As a result, there will eventually be probably only a handful of big players on the Net. Those who establish themselves early will have an advantage. Those who do it right will have an advantage.

Sales on the Internet in the early days were mostly by companies that were "Internet companies." Like Amazon or CDNow, most retail stores on the Net were created specifically to exist on the Net. However, established companies, as they come to the Net, have many advantages over Internet companies. They are generally larger than online stores so have lots more money to work with. They have recognized brands. They are known and trusted entities. They can cross-promote their physical stores on the Net and their Web site in their physical store. They could offer in-store pickup of items ordered online for customers who wish to avoid shipping charges. They have a big advantage in customer service when there are local physical stores where one can easily return an online purchase or get it serviced. Macy's (http://www.macys.com), for example, allows customers to return items bought online to any of their brick and mortar stores.

The online battle for books between Amazon and Barnes and Noble shows, however, that there are significant advantages to being the first to market. Amazon dominates online book sales (80% market share) with offline giant Barnes and Noble's online sales amounting to only about 10% of Amazon's.

iPrint (http://www.iprint.com) was the first online printer. They offer unique interactive design and have been doing a booming business. They realized that competition would soon appear from established offline printing giants with far more money to invest. The approach of many start-ups in that situation would be to build brand identity on the Net as quickly as possible, so they are well established before the big offline printers appear as online competition. iPrint's strategy, however, was to work with the potential competitors. The iPrint capability is the print facility for the online versions of Office Max and Sir Speedy.

Creative Imitation

The company that is first into a market isn't necessarily the one that becomes the leader. It isn't necessarily the one that becomes first in the minds of the customers. Often, the first into the market doesn't get the product quite right, which leaves an opportunity for a follower to take away the leadership position. It is what Peter Drucker calls creative imitation in *Innovation and Entrepreneurship*. The Altair computer was the first commercially available personal computer. It was geeky: it had no keyboard, no display, no software. Customers had to be very technical to get anything out of an Altair, but it was a huge hit among technology students and engineers. The Apple II computer appeared later, was much easier to use than the Altair (and Altair's many imitators that had appeared), had a keyboard and lots of available software. Less technically sophisticated hobbyists could use an Apple II. That greatly enlarged the market. Apple took the leadership position from Altair. But when Apple II's started showing up in corporations, there was strong resistance from management and the IT staff. They were considered toys, inappropriate for business purposes. IBM stepped in with the IBM PC and legitimized the notion of a personal computer. Although the computer was not significantly better than an Apple II, it was much easier for corporations to buy from trusted IBM than from little upstart Apple. IBM moved the computer from a hobby market to a business market and took the leadership position from Apple.

Similar stories have happened online. There were lots of little bookstores before Amazon came along. But Amazon redefined what an online bookstore could be, offering millions of titles, and took the lead away from the little online shops. CDNOW did the same thing in entertainment CDs. But then when Amazon started selling CDs, which was very similar in structure to their book business, Amazon's strong brand took the lead in CD retailing away from CDNOW. Offline book retailing giant Barnes and Noble attempted to do to Amazon what IBM had done to Apple, but this time without success. The creative imitator must bring more to the market than the entrepreneur has. Barnes and Noble was going up against a lot of strength online.

Be First in a New Category

If an incumbent has already taken the first position in the minds of customers, a company newly entering a market may be able to define a new subcategory and be first in that. Miller did it with Lite beer. Budweiser dominated the beer category, so Miller created the Lite beer category and is still the dominant product.

Big players in the online book retailing business have such a strong lead that they would be difficult and expensive to displace. Barnes and Noble tried hard to displace Amazon from its number one position with little result. But new online book retailers continue to appear. eFollett.com sells college text books. Every book eFollett.com sells is available through Amazon.com or BarnesandNoble.com, so how can eFollett.com compete? The books don't differ, but the market does. When a student goes to a university bookstore, the bookstore has the books arranged course by course with flags indicating which are required and which are recommended reading. But there is no central university authority that the university bookstore goes to for the list of required books. The bookstore must do the legwork of contacting each professor on campus and getting his required book list. And that's how eFollet.com differentiates itself from the general online mega-bookstores like Amazon.com and Barnes-andNoble.com. At the eFollett.com site a student can choose from a list of colleges and universities across the country, then select the courses she's taking, then add the required books to her shopping cart. Recalling all those times fighting my way through crowded university bookstores a few days before classes began, I see a lot of value in ordering books online—a few clicks and it's time to get some beers!

Enter a term in a search engine and you get a list of results. The service is paid for by the banner ad at the top of the page, right? Well, there may be more to it than that. There may be additional links on the page that are paid placement. There may be links that look like navigation aids on the page but which are actually paid placement. The idea behind GoTo.com (http://www.goto.com) is to provide search where all the paid links are shown as such.

GoTo lists not only search results, but also a parenthetical remark stating how much GoTo is being paid to present the link. Businesses that want to promote their sites can bid on search words. Search results are sorted in order of bid amounts, highest bids at the top of the list. If a user clicks on a link, GoTo collects the bid amount from the Web site owner. Typical top ranking bids are only a few cents but "computers" went for $1/click-through, "lexus" went for $1.30 but the top-ranked link in the "mercedes" result page was merely a 38-cent bid. Unlike conventional search engines, GoTo.com gives Web site promoters a clear way to come out on top of the listings. In addition, the promoter only pays for results. No click-throughs, no cost.

The value of the search engine depends on whether users see value in it. Many apparently do since GoTo currently serves about 100 million searches per month. GoTo argues that full disclosure is a more efficient filter of sites when customers want to buy. Although it's an unusual business model for the Web, it's similar to perhaps the most popular pay-for-placement offline medium, the Yellow Pages.

Feel like there's no way to put new content on the Web? Feel like it's all been done before? Well, it's true that among the hundreds of millions of Web pages it's getting harder and harder to publish something novel and interesting. Learn2 (http://www.learn2.com) has taken an interesting approach: all its content is organized into "survival guides," brief step-by-step descriptions of how to accomplish hundreds of tasks. While the information itself may not be unique, the organization and presentation are unique.

Be Unchallengeable

You know that machine that resurfaces the ice for hockey games or figure skating events? What's that called? When I ask this question of seminar attendees, they invariably say, "Zamboni!" That's why I like to call the unchallengeable niche a Zamboni market. There aren't all that many ice rinks in the country, and each needs only one or two Zambonis. And the Zamboni is a specialized piece of equipment that would cost a potential competitor a significant investment to develop and produce. Is it worth trying to compete with Zamboni given its nearly 100% market share? Probably not.

Zamboni could open the market to competition if they demanded enormous profits or if they failed to take advantage of technological innovations. Aside from that, Zamboni's position appears secure.

WinningHabits.com is a Web site service for fitness clubs. The management of fitness clubs are typically not interested in Web site development or maintenance, but they are each pressured to have a Web presence. WinningHabits.com will build a Web site for a fitness club, fill it with lots of fitness and nutritional information, which is updated regularly, provide an online store for fitness clothing and gear, provide member newsletters by e-mail and discussion areas for the fitness club staff who, with odd shift hours, are hard to get together. The bill is charged on a per club member basis and is typically passed on to the club members as a fee of a few dollars per month. Fitness club owners get an excellent and frequently refreshed Web site with no hassle. Is the fitness club Web site market small enough for WinningHabits.com to build an unchallengeable position? That will depend on how fast they move to dominate and how far along they are by the time competitors consider entering the market.

Disruptive Opportunities

Occasionally, circumstances offer unique strategic opportunities. Examples are demographic shifts, social trends and major shifts in technology. When a company identifies and acts on one of these strategic opportunities before its competitors do, it can gain significant competitive advantage. It may also move into a new marketplace where competitors don't currently exist.

Disruptive opportunities share one important characteristic: They don't last long. Advantage goes to companies that recognize disruptive opportunities early and act decisively.

Fads come and go, but social trends are changes that persist. When a leadership company fails to recognize a social trend that affects its market, it may lose its leadership position to a company that focuses on the new trend. Athletic shoes before Nike were relatively basic: They had to have rubber soles and had to be washable. Nike re-engineered the running shoe for comfort and performance using new designs and new materials and a lot of experimentation. These high-tech shoes might have just been a niche market had not there been a coincident societal shift toward fitness and exercise, particularly running. Nike had the shoes that armies of runners needed to avoid injuries. The old-line athletic shoe companies were left flat-footed.

Disruptive architectures and technologies change the array of opportunities before customers and so may change the way customers do what they do. Not every technological innovation is disruptive, but when disruptive technologies appear, leadership companies are replaced in their leadership positions by an upstart challenger who better understands the implications of the new technology. Sun unseated Digital Equipment Corporation, the leader in engineering computing, by understanding the implications of non-proprietary hardware and software for computer architecture, client/server technology and networking, none of which was invented by Sun. Shugart with its 8" disk drive, popular in minicomputers, replaced Burroughs and IBM, the dominant companies building 14" drives. Seagate with its 5.25" drives, popular in desktop computers, replaced Shugart.

Conner replaced Seagate as the leader with 3.5" drives, popular in laptop computers.

Leadership companies have great advantages over their competition. But leadership is theirs to lose. They may self-destruct through mismanagement. Collins' and Porras' *Built To Last* provide cautionary examples from Zenith, Howard Johnson and Burroughs.

Top management changes in a leading company may create a disruptive strategic opportunity if an appropriate successor has not been prepared. The decline of Zenith Corporation following the death of its domineering founder, "Commander" Eugene F. McDonald, Jr. is attributed to the absence of an appropriately prepared successor. If a leadership company is dominated by one individual (Bill Gates at Microsoft leaps to mind), one wonders if the company could maintain its leadership without that individual.

A leading company could fail to build for its future. Howard Johnson focused on cost control rather than innovation and missed the segmentation of the restaurant and hotel business. Marriott assumed the leadership position.

A leading company could self-destruct by stifling innovation. Burroughs was the leading computer company in 1960. It was headed by Ray W. Macdonald, who drove away risk takers and publicly humiliated managers for failures and mistakes. Burroughs failed to move decisively into business computing, despite its technological leadership. Through the 1960s Burroughs lost its leadership to IBM and its IBM 360 series of business computers. While IBM was developing the 360, one of the most audacious gambles in business history, Macdonald described Burroughs as working on improving profitability.

Consumer networking services Compuserve, Prodigy, Genie, Delphi and others disappeared or were entirely reformed just as a large number of people began to go online. Shouldn't these have been boom times? These companies were caught in the shift—partly technological, partly social—from proprietary networks to the open networking of the Internet. They failed to make the transition. The transition was not impossible to make, however. Not only did America Online make the transition, but it has prospered. Today it is the most powerful online brand. Was it easy? No. It had to change its pricing structure from hourly access charges to flat monthly fees, go through a very difficult period of explosive growth, which temporarily resulted in very poor service, and provide easy access to the information on the Internet rather than see that as a threat to its own information sources within the proprietary network.

10 Product and Service

Intel's latest Pentium® III processors are manufactured using the advanced 0.18-micron process. This new generation of technology brings all the performance-enhancing features of the Pentium III processor into exciting new PC products. For the Desktop, the Intel® Pentium® III processor is now available at 1.0 GHz (1000 MHz). Available for both desktop and mobile users, the redesigned Pentium III processor with Advanced Transfer Cache means you have all the power and performance for today's and tomorrow's Internet applications.

— Intel, selling on product
features and technology

Product Features

The value offered by Amazon's service as a book retailer is in its features. 1-Click Ordering, order status, order history, order confirmation e-mails, order shipment e-mails, quick response of pages, professional book reviews, customer book reviews, recommendations of similar books, e-mailed alerts about new releases by author or book category, special occasion reminders, gift wish lists and digital gift certificates. Although many of these features are common on other shopping sites, some are not. Also, the entire collection of features and the quality execution of the features sets Amazon apart.

Features of the shopping service also differentiate the shopping experience at Garden.com. The Design a Garden application and online garden club discussions make shopping at the site more enjoyable.

Applications are becoming more common over the Net and that feature alone is often promoted as a differentiator. TurboTax (http://www.turbotax.com) is available for tax preparation over the Web. The headline on the page is, "Do your taxes online!" It eliminates the hassle of installing tax software on one's own computer when it will probably be used for a day or two, then never used again. Most software titles, however, have difficulty competing with the speed and convenience of applications resident on one's own PC. Nevertheless, some applications are ideally suited to networking and these are becoming more common as online applications.

BidCom (http://www.bidcom.com) has a construction project management system on the Net. The product is differentiated from other project management software by its being on the Web, available for access by any of the participants. The system supports workflow through the entire process of building a building. It ties together contractors, the customer, suppliers, everyone involved in the complex process of construction. Each individual accessing the site gets a personalized view of the process showing what he's done and which tasks he has to do. This system aggregates and integrates information across many businesses into one coherent construction management system. And since the application runs on the network, it puts very little IT burden on the small businesses that need to participate. Perhaps some day we'll all pay per use for wordprocessors and spreadsheets that run on the Net; but in the meantime we'll see more network-based applications like BidCom's.

Great and changing content brings visitors. Consistent quality of content differentiates ZDNet's product from potential competitors. Ziff-Davis publishes more than a dozen computer magazines. In addition to printing, it publishes them online at ZDNet (http://www.zdnet.com). ZDNet also includes discussions, software downloads, product comparisons and ZD University, a Web-based learning center. And all the material is about computing. Because of this focus, ZDNet's content not only builds traffic, but traffic of people interested in computers. That bit of intelligence is worth a lot to advertisers, which is why ZDNet can charge nearly ten times as much for ads as can general sites like Yahoo.

The product sold at Sportsline is advertising exposure. One of the differentiating features of their product is the length of time each exposure lasts, which increases an ad's effectiveness. Longer exposure means higher click-through rates. The sports sites do it with live scores. Go to one of the sports sites (such as Sportsline at http://www.sportsline.com/u/sportsticker/scoreboard/mlbsbd.htm) and pull up a page of scores. Wait a while. The page and all scores are updated every minute or so. The idea is for sports fans to keep this page on their browsers all day long to keep abreast of the scores in all games as they happen.

Like Sportsline, Gamesville sells advertising, which is differentiated by uncommonly long exposures to ads. Gamesville (http://www.gamesville.com) offers continually refreshed content: It consists of the play of free online games enhanced by the lure of cash prizes. The cash prizes are minimal, but they seem to be sufficient to draw a lot of players.

Gamesville is funded by advertising. Ads appear during the play of a game, but more important, they appear in the 2 to 4 minutes between games. The players tend to read these ads since many players are just waiting for the next game to begin anyhow. The click-through rate on ads is uncommonly high, as much as 10%.

Be the Solution

Is it better to sell wedding dresses or help brides solve the problem of putting together the entire wedding event? Is it better to offer software product reviews or sell products? How many businesses must an aspiring online entrepreneur work with in order to get his store in business? One way that companies differentiate their offerings is defining themselves, not in terms of the products they sell—bridal gowns, software or Web site design—but in terms of the problem they solve for the customer.

The Knot (http://www.theknot.com) is a "with it" bridal shop. Through their Web site they strive to offer a "complete solution" for brides. Tons of content (over 3,000 articles), community through chat and message boards, calculators and other planning tools, and a complete selection of wedding gowns: over 8,000 to choose from. This sort of store simply couldn't exist in the offline world.

Not everything they have tried has worked. They tried an online sitcom about a bride and groom to be. "Our users couldn't have cared less." This is consistent with the notion of being the wedding solution: The online sitcom doesn't help solve the bride's problem. Leave it out.

One of the most popular and useful sections of computer magazines like *Macworld* is the product reviews. But now, with online versions of magazines, does it make sense to separate reviews from sales? New technologies call for new strategies. Macbuy marries the objective and reliable lab-tested reviews by the premier Macintosh authority *Macworld* with the convenience of pricing and immediate buying from the top authorized industry resellers. Macbuy.com (http://www.macbuy.com) gives consumers the right buying information the first time and expert advice on making the best purchase decisions, not just slick marketing. It's a one-stop, interactive center designed and continually developed with the consumer in mind.

I'm often asked what is the easiest way to set up a store online. It doesn't get much easier than VStore (http://www.vstore.com). VStore allows one to create a store by selecting a few look-and-feel parameters, handles the credit card processing and takes care of fulfillment. It even provides the products! Aspiring retailers need only check off the product categories they'd like their store to carry, and those products will appear in the store. There are hundreds of product categories to choose from, hundreds of thousands of products. Does the retailer lose some control over his store? Sure. But if easy is what you're looking for, it doesn't get much easier than this.

Think of an online retailer with an affiliate program. A really great affiliate program that even designs Web pages for you. Now, eliminate the retailer's online store leaving just the affiliate network. That's pretty much what Vstore is. It's like Amazon.com without the Amazon Web site.

Auxiliary Services

Books are an ultimate commodity product. No matter where one buys a book, the book is the same as it would be if it were bought anywhere else. How can an online bookstore differentiate itself from other online bookstores when they all offer the same books? The stores differentiate themselves with auxiliary services. Amazon.com features reviews by readers and interviews with authors. BarnesandNoble.com features frequent chat sessions with popular authors. When viewing a book, Amazon lists other books that customers who have ordered this book have also ordered. Both have book recommendation services based on a customer's stated interests and based on his behavior: the books he's bought. Amazon and BarnesandNoble have nearly matched one another service for differentiating service, so they no longer differentiate. The two leaders are not far apart. However, the services those two offer have significantly differentiated them from the rest of the competition.

Coastal Tool (http://www.coastaltool.com), probably the leading power tool online store, built their business and reputation on great customer service. Their Tool Doctor answers questions within 24 hours. But as their online business grew, the number of questions grew as well, including lots of questions that were unlikely to lead to sales for Coastal Tool. What to do?

The most common questions were about getting local service on power tools. Coastal Tool put together an extensive database of power tool manufacturers' local service centers and made the list available through their Web site. Service center questions dropped from about 50/day to one or two per day. Better service, less work.

You might have a wonderful product, but it doesn't matter unless your customers are motivated to do something about the problem you solve. That's the beauty of the Position Agent (http:// positionagent.bcentral.com/). They help companies improve their position on search engines. To motivate the need for their service, they offer the Position Agent service. You type in your URL and the term you'd like people to find you with. The Position Agent then checks ten search engines and tells you if you came up in the top 10 or even the top 200 hits. You didn't show as well as you'd like? Now maybe you're interested in their service.

One of the early demonstrations on the Web was a currency converter. It was a free service by some dedicated soul. Thomas Cook Travel (http://www.us.thomascook.com/convert.htm) has figured out how to make money from the idea. They offer a free currency converter calculator on their Web site but then take it to the next step: Users can buy some of the foreign currency and have it mailed to them.

That's a great idea! It's always a hassle to have to exchange some currency in the airport upon arrival so you at least have cab fare to your hotel. It would be a great convenience to have some local currency before the trip begins.

Do on the Net what the Net is good at doing. That seems to be the idea behind Egghead's new online store (http://www.egghead.com). What's the Net good at doing? Large inventories (30,000 products offered), auctions, time-sensitive sales (surplus and liquidation sales offered), software downloads. Egghead offers it all.

What else could they have done? Frequent buyer credits, e-mail notification when certain surplus products are available, suggestive selling, more info on designing solutions (like networking your office) similar to what Garden.com does for designing gardens or links to customer support info similar to what Coastal Tools does for power tools. Egghead.com is differentiating itself from other online computer retailers with the range of services it offers.

International Golf Outlet (http://www.igogolf.com) offers golfing products over the Net. One of their most popular services is custom-fitted clubs. Typically, custom fitted clubs are fitted by a golf pro for $50-$100. IGO offers a similar service for free. Request the custom-fitting form through their Web site and answer about 20 questions. IGO experts then analyze the results and suggest the clubs that would work best. Why offer this service for free? "This brings us a ton of business," says David Schofman, founder of IGO.

The Personal Calendar is a new category to the ranks of free Web-based services. The likes of Day-Timer (http://www.daytimer.com) and When.com (http://www.when.com/) offer Web users a chance to keep personal or group calendars online at no charge. Not only that, but they supply a fairly extensive collection of events that are easy to schedule into your own calendar. Book releases, chat events, broadcasts, movies, cultural events, sporting events and on and on. Very nice, free and likely to get better with time.

How do they make money? The banner ads pay some of the bills. Day-Timer can think of the Web site as a way to improve and promote their paper planners. But there's another opportunity here: transactions.

The calendar sites make it easy and convenient to pull a commercial event into your busy future. And when you're thinking about where to go and what to do, it ought to be possible to buy a ticket for the event. Why not? The link could be right there. The revenue for the calendar site is generated through referral fees for the transaction. So one could think of When.com as an innovative front-end for Ticketmaster.

In their book *Blur*, Davis and Meyer suggest that among the changes in business these days is the blurring distinction between products and services. Traditionally, a book has been a product. They are trying to make it a service as well by creating a corresponding Web site. Throughout the book readers are invited to the Web site. The site (http://www.blursight.com) offers more up-to-date information as well as an opportunity for readers to participate and add their own idea and stories.

Not sure what that sweater from the online catalog will look like on you? At Lands End (http://www.landsend.com) you can now try it on. Their Personal Model takes several parameters—hair color, height, shoulders, waist, hips, waist placement—then builds a model to those specifications. The model can then try on clothes to see if they're right. Of course, the model can be saved in a personal account, a feature that would encourage shoppers to come back. Lands End also offers advice on which clothes flatter a person with the given parameters and they offer personalized fashion advice. It's too bad for those of us who really need this service. It's currently available only for women.

Unique Skills, Knowledge, Experience

Eric Ward of The WardGroup/NetPost is known for his skills at promoting Web sites, which is what differentiates his service from the competition. He knows how to make use of the Net's resources to get articles placed, how to get links to a site installed and how to generate buzz about a site in discussion groups. Service companies like Ward's thrive on their unique skills, knowledge and experience. The same applies to much larger service companies like Andersen Consulting. And it applies to product companies: We'd trust an airliner built by Boeing but may demand extra assurances before flying in one of Joe's Pretty Good Jumbo Jets.

Many online businesses start with a Web site and then try to promote it. For Tim Carter, things went in the other direction. He was named by *Remodelling* magazine as one of the 50 top remodellers in the country. He built on that recognition, first with a newspaper column, then with radio and TV shows and now with a Web site (http://www.askthebuilder.com). One of the benefits of the media exposure is each appearance is another opportunity for promotion. He's been promoting his Web site and uses the content from the columns and shows as content for the site.

All this exposure (and great content) has built his Web traffic. He now sells ad space on his site for about five times the rate of general sites.

Technology

Product differentiation often evokes the notion of "a better mouse-trap." These days, technology is often the source of improved performance, so it is often the source of product differentiation.

Real.com has developed technology for delivering and playing streaming audio and streaming video across the Internet. Their technology (in addition to their marketing methods) has differentiated Real from the competition, helping to make them the leader in providing software for real time media across the Net. Technology was the source of their differentiation. Then aggressively building market share and making their technology the one most commonly used has made the advantage sustainable.

The culture of the Net is about moving bits around for free. Sharing bits with friends. But what if those bits happen to be copyrighted material such as video clips, interactive animations or cartoon characters? Some property owners attempt to quash the enthusiasm of their fans by claiming that since cartoon images and TV show clips are copyrighted, it is a copyright violation to distribute them. But this strategy attacks their most enthusiastic fans. Surely there's a better way.

ThingWorld (http://www.thingworld.com) is about enabling people to give "things" away yet still maintain some control over them. The "things" can only be viewed if a free thingviewer has been downloaded and installed. The technology advantage is that the "things" are relatively tamperproof: Links and other properties are kept intact. The things get distributed and they can still drive commerce by linking back to catalogs or Web sites. They may even encourage repeat visits as fans return to complete their collections of things.

How does your Web site stack up against the competition? It's a lot of work to figure that out but WebCriteria (http://www.webcriteria.com) now makes the job easier. They offer free ongoing studies of leading Web sites in ten markets. The studies compare load times, freshness of content, composition (text versus graphics) and accessibility (how long it takes to reach different parts of the site). You can also pay for custom studies to compare your site with the competition. The technology WebCriteria has developed for site analysis differentiates them from the competition.

Customization

The point of product differentiation is to provide customers with products that better fit their needs. The ultimate in differentiated products are customized products.

Every computer that Dell (http://www.dell.com) sells is built to order. There is no extra fee for customization; it's just how Dell does business.   When placing an order at the Dell Web site, the customer can specify processor, memory, disk, display, video memory, video card, DVD, CDROM, sound card, speakers, modem, Internet access, Zip drive, operating system, bundled software, antivirus software, keyboard, joysticks, mouse, networking card, support contract, tape drive, floppy drive, printer, scanner, power protection training and other installed software.

I was recently in a hurry to get a notebook computer to use in a seminar, but it needed fairly high-end capabilities. I was going to be using it not only to show Web pages and PowerPoint slides, but also to store and play several hours worth of video clips. I needed a notebook with a very large disk and a lot of video memory and I needed it fast. I raced from computer store to computer store around Dallas, looking for one that fit the bill, but found none. I had about three weeks until my seminar and decided to risk a custom order at Dell for my dream computer. I paid a premium for the unusual features I needed but eliminated anything that wouldn't be needed. The three-week time frame was not a problem—I received the custom computer three days later.

Personal Passions (http://www.personalpassions.com) and YourNovel.com (http://www.yournovel.com) offer customized romance novels in much the same way that Dell offers customized computers. The would-be romance author fills out a form of about sixty items about himself and his or her love interest and selects how steamy the novel should be. A few days later the bound novel appears in the mail ready to revitalize a romance!

State of the Art Kids (http://www.sotakids.com) offers customized books for kids.

Several Web sites now offer custom clothing. Nike (http://www.nike.com) offers the NikeID line of shoes, which include a personal ID of up to 8 characters on the back of the shoe. ActionFit (http://www.actionfit.com) offers custom swim suits and aerobic wear, Country Road Fashions (http://www.countryroadfashions.com) offers custom Western wear and Interactive Custom Clothes Company (http://www.ic3d.com) offers custom jeans in over a hundred fabrics. Then there are custom knit hats from Yossel's Toessels (http://www.toessel.com) who claim to be "saving the world of knitting from weenies with hats that could kick yer butt."

Customer Service

One of the most well-known (because it was first) examples of differentiating customer service across the Net was that of FedEx offering automatic package tracking through their Web site. It replaced the cost of tracking through 800 number phone calls. The original site, which cost $50,000 to implement and $50,000 to promote, paid for itself by saving the equivalent of $125,000 in phone calls *in its first month of operation!* Not only did it save money, but it improved customer satisfaction.

Package tracking is available on the Web sites of all the major overnight and parcel services. CSX (http://www.csx.com) has taken the idea a step further. When customers ship on CSX rail lines, they can access the CSX Web site to take care of nearly any need that arises. Customers can obtain shipment status for user-defined pools, corporate fleets and individual cars, monitor shipment tracking through a graphical map, create and submit bills of lading, contact other users and CSX through their bulletin board, place car orders for future needs, submit freight claims, manage pools of equipment, analyze price information, query physical equipment specifications, view waybills, or submit yard management inquiries, requests and modifications.

In other words, if you do business with CSX you can probably do it through their Web site. The system has been a big hit with customers bringing over 400,000 inquiries per month.

When browsing on most retail Web sites, you are on your own. Not so at 1-800-Flowers (http://www.1800flowers.com). Their eQ&A chat allows customers to chat with store representatives in real time through the Web site. The store representatives can serve about half a dozen simultaneous conversations (although you'd think the representatives would start to get confused!). And that makes chat-based customer service cheaper than 800 number-based customer service.

Of five prominent navigation links on the Ski Europe site (http://www.ski-europe.com), one is *Have a Question?* Why give so much attention to the ability to ask a question? They found that visitors who were engaged in e-mail exchanges with the company were three times more likely to buy than the average.

Most Web sites offer a way to send feedback to the Webmaster or to ask a question about content. But if simply facilitating communication is an effective means for closing sales, perhaps it should be strongly promoted on other sites.

My computer crashed yesterday. After restarting, the mouse no longer worked. I visited the Logitech site (http://www.logitech.com) hoping for enlightenment in their online troubleshooting guide, but it provided no useful information for my problem.

Lesson 1: If you're going to have an online troubleshooting guide, make it extensive enough to be useful. Otherwise, you're just teasing and frustrating your customers.

Not knowing what else to do, I attempted to fill out a customer support form asking for help; but they required so much information about model numbers, serial numbers, processor type, amount of RAM and on and on, I was stymied.

Lesson 2: If you don't want customer e-mails, require lots of obscure data that you don't even need.

Lesson 2a: If you don't want customer e-mails yet you want happy customers, improve your self-help capability (see Lesson 1).

Rather than find all that stuff, I figured I'd just reinstall the mouse drivers—maybe that would work. I downloaded the latest drivers, installed them and everything now works as it should.

Lesson 3: If your product requires support software, make it available on your site for free. Your customers will appreciate it and your products will work better for them.

Product catalogs and FAQs are good, but sometimes customers just need to ask a simple question. E-mail is easy to implement for questions but has the disadvantage, from the customer's point of view, of not being real time. Would you rather have your question answered now or later? But real time chat systems are much more complex to implement than e-mail.

LivePerson (http://www.liveperson.com) offers a chat application service across the Net. With LivePerson, your site appears to have an integrated chat server. Actually, the chat is being run on LivePerson's server. Your customer may be talking to one of your own customer service representatives (the most common case), or LivePerson can provide customer service representatives to answer questions about your products. Either way, live chat is a way to resolve customers' questions and move them closer to buying in real time.

Convenience

One of the hot ideas in e-commerce these days is the notion of the *infomediary*, an agent who collects information for the benefit of consumers. The ultimate infomediary, which knows all about a consumer's needs, wants and preferences, as well as about all the available products that could fill those needs, is a long way off. However, many steps in that direction have been taken.

One of the first steps in consumer advocacy is simply making choices available to the customer. The power of the Net to provide choice is best exemplified by those businesses that provide "everything" in a market through their stores. Amazon (http://www.amazon.com) was one of the first to do this by providing millions of book titles. Amazon was able to offer far more titles through their online store than any physical bookstore could. This range of titles enabled customers to find and select the books they wanted with fewer constraints imposed by the bookseller.

Breadth

Last week I was looking for a wireless phone. Ordinarily, I start my shopping on the Net, but I happened to be in a local mall, so I stopped in a store and found just what I was looking for: wireless, 2-lines, caller ID, headset connector. But the price was high, $260. So I tried Yahoo!Shopping (http://shopping.yahoo.com) when I got home. Yahoo!Shopping is one of several online store aggregators on the Net. Yahoo! provides search and access to the products of lots of stores. It's an easy way to search for features and compare prices without going to lots of stores. And one can typically find low prices: 35-45% off is not unusual.

But this has been around for a long time in the form of mail order catalogs. So what's new? A couple of differences stand out.

The Net includes thousands of catalogs available for shopping at any time. Compare that with having the equivalent paper catalogs mailed to your house and hanging on to them until you're ready to buy.

Services like Yahoo!Shopping aggregate the contents of the online catalogs. In essence, I was able to create my own "catalog" on the fly from many stores of wireless 2-line phones with caller ID and a headset jack.

Savings? I bought the identical phone I had seen in the mall for $170 instead of $260, a 35% savings.

One of the unique advantages of online stores is their ability to offer a great selection of products. Amazon first demonstrated the idea by offering millions of books. Ashford.com (http://www.ashford.com) is following suit. Ashford offers luxury products, including over 7,000 styles of luxury watches (no Timexes here). That many watches would take a lot of expensive showcase space in a physical store or a thick and costly catalog for a mail order business. But large product breadth can be readily handled online and offers significant differentiation between online stores and their offline competitors.

What can an online store offer that a physical store can't? One answer is breadth in the form of enormous inventory. That was the original appeal of Amazon books and many others. It's also the appeal of Discount Games (http://www.discountgames.com), which carries an inventory of more than 20,000 items, most of which are adventure game miniatures. Although it's actually more expensive to sell and ship these products over the Net, customers appreciate the breadth of choice and convenience of the online store.

Blockbuster and Hollywood Entertainment dominate the video rental business in the U.S. Want to rent a video? Drive over to the video store, pick one out and pop it into the VCR. Reel.com (http://www.reel.com) has been an online video sales and rental store as well as an offline, bricks and mortar store. They did a couple of things the big players didn't, in addition to being online: They offered about 85,000 titles rather than a few thousand, and they constructed The

Movie Guide, an extensive movie recommendation database of personally selected recommendations (not just mechanical queries).

Hollywood is out to overtake market leader Blockbuster, so they're looking for innovations. They must have decided Reel.com is one because they recently bought them and will soon be offering access to The Movie Guide through kiosks in their stores as well as augmenting their offering with online sales and rentals of Reel's extensive title list.

Disintermediation and Reintermediation

Disintermediation means cutting out the middleman. That is what Dell is doing by selling direct from manufacturer to end customer: cutting out the retailer. It's what the airlines do when selling tickets on their Web sites rather than through travel agents. It's also what online retailers like Netmarket (http://www.netmarket.com) do when they make agreements with manufacturers to drop ship goods from the factory that have been ordered through the Netmarket storefront. In the case of Netmarket, the intermediary that is being eliminated is often the distributor.

The issue of distribution is that manufacturers produce a large quantity of a small number of products. Consumers each purchase a small number of a large number of products. The first function of retailing is aggregating products from lots of manufacturers for consumers, and then selling the products in small quantities. But the aggregation portion of that function is primarily an information task, which is why we are seeing the Net have an impact on distribution.

Another form of disintermediation occurs when information that was once closely held suddenly becomes widely available.   Investment advice is an example.   Stockbrokers had access to research on stocks that was not easily available to the general public, from research reports to real time quotes on stock prices.   They used this information to give investment advice to their clients, then would execute trades for them and charge about $200.   Discount brokerages started offline by offering only the trades, not the advice.   The discount broker business took off with the Internet because of the easy access to research information, stock quotes and investment discussions.   The Net changed the value of the broker's advice.

Real estate agents are in a situation similar to stockbrokers.   Listings of available properties, once held closely by the agents, are now available online.   Information about local school districts, nearby shopping and neighborhood recreational facilities are also available online, as is comparative data on available mortgage rates.   The availability of all this information reduces the incentive of the seller to list his house with a Realtor and reduces the incentive of a buyer to buy through a Realtor when buyers and sellers consider the cost: typically 6% of the price of the property.   The transition away from Realtors is likely to move fairly slowly, however, for another reason: Buying a house is usually the largest investment a family will make, and it can be comforting to be guided through the process by an experienced agent.   But is it worth 6%?   Perhaps in time the Realtor will become more of a real estate therapist.

In spite of the examples above, it is a mistake to assume that all the changes in distribution will result in disintermediation. New intermediaries are appearing as old ones disappear. The Net is causing a reshuffling of distribution. Consider shopping aggregators like Yahoo!Shopping (http://shopping.yahoo.com) allowing comparisons of products across thousands of stores and millions of products. Yahoo!Shopping does not cut out a middleman; it adds a new one— a retailer of retailers. But in doing so, it adds value by making comparisons much easier than visiting many stores individually and it does so at low cost—a transaction fee which participating stores absorb as a marketing cost.

Vehicle purchase has also been reintermediation. In the past, auto dealerships held all the information power. They knew what cars cost, what options cost, what financing cost and what trade-in vehicles were worth. Unless a buyer put forth strenuous effort, she was dealing in an information vacuum. Today, online companies like AutobyTel (http://www.autobytel.com) provide a wealth of information on new and used vehicles, insurance rates, availability, financing and more. At this point, however, the online automotive sites do not replace dealers; they aggregate dealers much like Yahoo!Shopping does. After a buyer has done her research she asks for fixed bids (no negotiation after the fact) on the car she wants, which AutobyTel then forwards to dealers.

The online dealerships currently perform the function of information source and negotiator for the buyer. The physical dealerships serve as a location to look at, purchase and take delivery of the vehicle. But vehicles could be looked at and test driven elsewhere, such as at car rental agencies. Purchase and delivery could take place at the buyer's home. If some rental car companies will bring the car to the customer for merely a rental, cars could be delivered for sale.

Finally, the transaction could take place between the customer and the manufacturer. What is reintermediation today could become disintermediation tomorrow.

11 Buyer Characteristics

Now there's a place where women don't just read about how they can get the most out of life, but can help each other do it. It's called iVillage.com: The Women's Network.

— iVillage.com Welcome page

Demographics, Psychographics, Individual Preferences

iVillage (http://www.ivillage.com) is one of the leading Web sites devoted to women's issues. KoreaLink is a popular service for connecting Koreans worldwide. MountainZone is for anyone interested in activities in the mountains. NetZero provides customers with free Internet access in exchange for tracking their online behavior and exposing ads to them based on what they do. Online businesses have unprecedented opportunities to tailor their offerings to people based on where they live, their income, their nationality, their interests and their behavior. And tailoring can be more precise than ever before, commonly down to individual preferences. Individualized services such as the My Yahoo! custom page are now commonplace and used by millions of individuals.

Advertisers would love to be able to show ads only to those people who want to see them. Sites that collect information on individual customers can have a pretty good idea of which customers are likely to be interested in which new products. But what about people who aren't your customers? Typically, the best we can do is advertise at sites that are likely to attract some of the kinds of people we're likely to want to sell to.

What would happen if each of us had a unique digital ID that indexed all sorts of data about our individual likes and dislikes? And what if the info about these likes and dislikes was collected from behavior not at one site but from sites all over the Net? It would be a boon to advertisers. And it's started with Firefly Passport (http://www.firefly.com), VeriSign's Digital ID and Microsoft's Global User ID.

Of course, the dark side of this approach is the potential privacy risks.

Specialization by Industry

Specializing on a particular segment of customers can allow services specifically for them and thereby differentiate their offering. Amazon.com and BarnesandNoble.com each offer millions of books, including university textbooks. University textbook online stores such as Textbooks.com and eFollett.com can differentiate themselves while selling books already available from Amazon and BarnesandNoble. The textbook companies accumulate lists of required texts from college professors. The textbook lists draw students to the online textbook stores.

Ours is a time of smaller and smaller market segments. The hot idea in achieving "stickiness" on a site is to make it into a portal, so Yahoo became, not just a directory, but access into anything you might need on the Web: information, chat, stores, free e-mail, live broadcasts and so on. The same with the other search engines. Then came vertical portals that focus on specific industries. It was the same idea as the Yahoo-style mass-market portals but more specific. Now we're seeing narrower horizontal portals like JustSell.com (http://www.justsell.com), a portal for sales people across industries.

Surely this subdivision will continue, but at some point it will meet a trend coming from the other direction: personalized versions of portals (like My Yahoo). With proper design, narrow horizontal and vertical portals could turn out to be no more than personalized views consisting of preselected subsets of the general portals. "Proper design," however, is easier said than done. There is now an opportunity for narrow portals to establish themselves before the general portals get the design right.

Geographic Location

In the physical world, location is a prime differentiator among retail stores. But on the Web, location means nothing: Every store is just a click away. Location is important, however, where the virtual world meets the real world. One can order office supplies from OfficeDepot.com, for example. If one chooses to return a purchase, it can be returned at any local Office Depot store without having to pay shipping charges.

One can now find several mapping sites on the Net. Put in a location and get a local street map. Generally these are funded by either advertising or corporate sponsorship. A corporate sponsor supplies a list of locations, any one of which could be clicked on to bring up a local map.

MapBlast (http://www.mapblast.com) is a similar mapping service that adds route planning and a client's database of locations. A company can provide customers with route planning, showing the locations of their franchises along the way as well as national parks, historic monuments and other locations of interest. And once a customer has used MapBlast to plan his route, the results, including the database of businesses along the way, can be downloaded onto his palmtop computer for the trip.

Corporate Web sites are becoming one of the most effective channels for finding new recruits for high tech companies. One difficulty I've experienced when recruiting in Dallas is that candidates often have higher offers from other parts of the country. One could argue that the cost of living is lower in Dallas than, say, Silicon Valley, but specific data was often not available. Now it is. Point your job candidates (and your HR department) to the Salary Calculator on the HomeFair.com site (http://www2.homefair.com/calc/salcalc.html). It compares equivalent salaries for cities around the world. It shows, for example, that a salary of $100,000 in Dallas, Texas is equivalent to $159,000 in San Jose, California.

12 Operations

*The modern car is almost unimaginably compli-
cated. A typical model is made up of more than
10,000 parts, each of which must be designed
and made by someone. Organizing this enormous task is probably the greatest challenge in
manufacturing a motor vehicle. Yet it is the one
least understood and appreciated by the outside
world.*

— Womack, Jones and Roos,
on Coordinating the Supply Chain
from *The Machine That Changed the World*

Coordination

Coordinating activities across corporate departments or across companies is a matter of information and policy. Coordination is one
thing the Net can do really well and many companies are using it to
their competitive advantage. We have already discussed several
examples. Cisco Systems outsources the production of their routers
(see pp. 65 and 92.) They gain a cost advantage worth hundreds of
millions of dollars per year. Dell Computer works very closely with
their parts suppliers. They have been able to differentiate their
business by radically reducing the funds tied up in parts inventory

and being more responsive to changing customer preferences and available technologies (see p. 105). Many online stores are able to present large product catalogs to their customers through the use of virtual inventory, which is another name for close coordination between a store and its suppliers. Coordinating to offer virtual inventories has enabled Netmarket and Amazon (see p. 43) to offer much larger product inventories than would be possible otherwise. A gardening superstore like Garden.com (see p. 64) offering 20,000 items, mostly live goods, simply could not exist without virtual inventory and close coordination with growers.

An illustration of just how much networks facilitate coordination between stores and their suppliers is the ease with which people sell products through affiliate programs described below (see p. 226). By simply adding special hyperlinks to Web pages, hundreds of thousands of sites have become e-businesses.

In the past, sales took orders, fulfillment shipped product, but the salesman, the point of contact, may not have been able to able to tell a customer if his order had been shipped. That is a lack of coordination. Online stores like CDNow not only take orders, but commonly also provide individual customer order histories so customers can see what has been ordered, what has shipped and what is still backordered.

Coordination across corporate lines tends to blur where one company ends and the other begins. Tight coordination can lead to long-term relationships between buyer and supplier. Staples.com, for example, is linked into the intranets of major customers, making them the corporate online office supplies supplier.

Ridout Plastics (http://www.ridoutplastics.com) offers custom plastic fab-rication services, a business-to-business sale. They only intend their Web site to be a brochure for their services. Orders are still taken offline, over the telephone.

How do they know how effective the Web site is? They could poll each customer when taking each order, but there's a less intrusive way: the toll free number given on the Web site is reserved for the Web site. Count the calls on that line and they know how many calls were generated by the Web site.

Scope

As companies build relationships with individual customers, the no-tion of share of market is being replaced by share of customer. Share of market is the fraction of customers in a market who buy from a particular vendor. Share of customer is the fraction of an individual customer's purchases that are from a particular vendor. Thinking in terms of share of customer is attractive because selling more to a known customer tends to be far less expensive than finding new customers. Scope is the range of products and services a company offers. Broader scope is often motivated by the desire to increase share of customer. Amazon.com has extended their offerings from books to books, music, video, toys and games, electronics, auctions and more. Amazon has millions of customers and these new depart-ments are an attempt to differentiate the company by scope, to sell each of those customers more products.

Yahoo! (http://www.yahoo.com) started out just as a directory service, funded by advertising. It's trying to expand now by including product sales, among many other things. It could enhance revenues with a slice of each transaction. But what does that do to its advertising? Is it cutting into the business of the companies that now pay the bills through ads? Will they decide to pull their ads due to the unwelcome competition?

Yahoo's traffic is primarily driven by the value of the directory. Its strategic question is now, can it better profit from that traffic through ads or through sales? It probably won't be able to do both in the long run.

Dell Computer is one of the most successful businesses on the Net. The match is nearly ideal: they've always sold direct and they let buyers custom-configure each computer; perfect for online sales. As of this writing, they're selling about $40 million online per day.

Computer buyers, Dell's customers, typically buy a computer only every few years. How should Dell use its great brand recognition on the Web, yet avoid diluting the brand? They've opened a companion store, Gigabuys.com (http://www.gigabuys.com). Unlike the computer sales, Gigabuys sells packaged goods, not custom. It helps Dell exploit its heavy traffic and great brand recognition between computer purchases. We should all have that problem!

SpringStreet (http://www.springstreet.com) lists over 7 million apartments available for rent in the U.S. It's a service free to Web visitors, funded by advertising. But if someone is looking for an apartment, what else do they need? Movers, furniture, possibly loans. In addition to ads for such services, SpringStreet now offers the opportunity to buy the services described on its site, usually at a reduced rate. The purchases are passed on to one of 35 partners and SpringStreet collects a transaction fee.

The Mountain Zone (http://www.mountainzone.com) strategy is built on Content, Commerce and Community. If it has to do with the mountains, it's in the Mountain Zone. With that idea in mind, they add over 200 pages to the site every day. The content is first divided up by mountain activity (snowboarding, mountain biking, hiking, skiing, photography), then by mountain locales. They also offer more than 6,000 products, all drop shipped, so they need carry no inventory themselves. Finally, their community consists of letters to the editor and e-mailed newsletters (a stretch of the definition of community; there is no real interaction among "community" members).

What's the key to Mountain Zone's success? They thoroughly serve the visitors who are interested in doing things in the mountains. They have a broad scope of resources and services for the mountain enthusiast.

Good stuff is often hard to find on the Net. That's why branding is becoming so important.

In the early days of the Net, it was thought that shopping malls would organize many stores into tidy bundles, making them easier to find for customers. Malls are a way in expand the scope of products offered and to co-promote stores by their collocation. Malls flopped. A few individual stores did very well, especially at growing their brand recognition. Amazon, Outpost.com and Beyond.com are outstanding examples. Now Amazon is extending that brand recognition to other stores (or departments within its store): music, electronics, software, toys, art, tools, lawn and patio, health and beauty, auctions and gifts in addition to books. This emerging department store has much in common with a shopping mall, but all the departments (stores) are under one brand.

Buy.com (http://www.buy.com) is doing the same thing. The Buy.com shopping portal provides access and consistent purchasing process and account history to (currently) eight stores: computers, software, games, music, videos, books, golf and clearance. The old idea of an Internet mall as nothing more than a page of links to stores is being replaced with the shopping portal, integrated stores with strong promotion and branding of the portal itself.

Scale

One of the biggest changes in business in the twentieth century was the development of mass production and the subsequent drop in consumer prices due to economies of scale. Economies of scale continue in the information age and scale is often a differentiator when choosing a vendor's services. In some cases customers are not seeking the *economy* of scale, but sheer scale—the ability to handle the big jobs. When a corporate customer, for example, wishes to provide real time streaming audio or video of its annual stockholders meeting, it must work with a company with the capacity to serve tens to hundreds of thousands of simultaneous viewers. High capacity providers like Yahoo!Broadcast (http://broadcast.yahoo.com) are differentiated from others by scale, the ability to do the big jobs.

There are thousands of Internet Service Providers (ISPs) throughout the country eager to host Web sites. But when high capacity sites need hosting, the ISP must be able to handle extraordinary volumes of traffic and provide extraordinary reliability. Microsoft, for example, gets millions of visitors to its Web site each day and many requests for product and driver downloads. The downloads of these large files are outsourced to ISPs that can handle the unusual volumes such as Conxion (http://www.conxion.com) and Exodus (http://www.exodus.com). The scale of jobs they can handle differentiates these ISPs from their competition.

Lots of small Web sites want to sell ad space, but the sites do not get enough traffic to interest large advertisers. Content aggregators like Digital Music Network (http://www.dmnmedia.com) collect the ad space selling potential of many related sites (music-oriented sites in the DMN example) and offer them to larger advertisers. Digital Music Network differentiates their service of selling ad space from that of the sites they aggregate by scale.

Intellectual Property

Priceline.com has a patent on its business model, name-your-own-price reverse auctions. Although patenting a business model is controversial, it is currently a point of difference between Priceline and the competition.

More traditional patents cover some of the technology used in e-businesses. For example, Amazon has a patent on its 1-Click Ordering process. Technology differentiators such as the technology behind streaming media, online buddy lists, supplier coordination technology typically are surrounded by patents as a means of creating a sustainable differentiation.

Speed

Speed is a difference that makes a difference to many Web surfers. If a Web site comes up slowly, many are unlikely to wait around long enough to make a purchase. And if a site is always fast, Yahoo! is an example, surfers are much more likely to return. In a recent test, eBay (http://www.ebay.com) auction pages were found to be fully rendered in about two seconds. One of its competitors averaged 16 seconds per page view. Surely the slower site is at a competitive disadvantage.

Beyond Web page speed, speed on task can be a strong differentiator. Yahoo!Shopping, for example, so greatly increases the speed of finding stores that offer products that many customers find it a convenient way to shop—in spite of the fact that it adds another level in the retail chain.

Buying books at Amazon.com through 1-Click Ordering is so quick and easy that I know I end up buying more books than I should. In fact, while working on the bibliography for this book I discovered I had multiple copies of some books. I wonder if there is a support group out there for folks like me with a 1-Click Ordering problem.

Loans once took days or weeks to process. Today, sites like LiveCapital.com take an application online, give an instant decision on the loan and present a list of lenders from which to compare and choose. A lending agency that took weeks to consider a loan would have to have a very compelling offer to overcome LiveCapital's speed advantage.

Partnerships

Jason Apfel wanted to start an online gift business like 1-800-FLOW-ERS. Flowers seemed to be taken; and, besides, it appeals almost exclusively as gifts for women. Instead, he selected fragrances and is now the leading online fragrance source. One of the benefits of fragrances is that it's a gift item that appeals to both men and women.

Four key ingredients contribute to FragranceNet's (http://www.fragrancenet.com) success. First, they offer the widest selection of brand name fragrances (no knockoffs)—about 1,000 brand names. Second, discount prices. Third, a close alliance with one of the largest fragrance distributors in the country, which makes their wide selection possible. Fourth, attention to customer service details. They offer a free gift with each purchase and follow up with a personal thank you note.

A set of exclusive partnerships is the most sustainable differentiator that Yahoo!Broadcast has, according to founder Mark Cuban. Before its acquisition by Yahoo! and before there was much competition in the Internet broadcast media market, Broadcast.com signed exclusive agreements with programming content sources such as radio stations, colleges and universities, sports teams and corporations. Now that Internet broadcast has become an accepted medium, Yahoo!Broadcast has a sustainable advantage over competitors.

13 Marketing and Sales

Be direct.

— Dell Computer

Channel Issues

Dell was ideally suited to sell its computers over the Net: It was a direct marketer (through mail order) and every computer it sold was customized, ordered before it was built to the customer's specifications. When Net commerce came along, Dell had no concerns about channel conflicts with retailers complaining about direct sales. Other computer companies (notably Compaq) have been plagued by channel conflict in their attempt to sell direct.

Do online stores need stock? Certainly someone needs to fill orders; but unlike offline stores, there may not be a need for online stores to stock any of the items it sells. Stores like NetMarket, which carries thousands of products, stocks nothing. Orders are passed on to manufacturers, who drop-ship products to customers. Online retail following this model saves on rent of expensive retail real estate, compared with offline stores, and can offer a vastly larger inventory of products.

A representative of barnesandnoble.com, the online spinoff of Barnes and Noble, said that the reason the online store is separate from the brick and mortar stores is because of sales tax. If the two were one company, the online store would have to collect sales tax on purchases shipped to every state because there are physical stores in every state. What does barnesandnoble.com lose by being separate from the offline stores? It misses out on the kinds of benefits that Eddie Bauer has gained by viewing the online store as another channel to market.

Eddie Bauer (http://www.eddiebauer.com), the Seattle-based clothing retailer, has done an excellent job of integrating their stores, catalogs and Net store. Their URL is on every page of the catalog (one of 120 million catalogs mailed annually). The online store offers a virtual dressing room, an interactive gift finder, gift reminder service and a wish list service. More sizes are available online and in the catalog than in the stores due to offline store stocking limitations. Stores have catalogs so customers can order products and sizes that aren't available in the store, and in-store catalog orders require no shipping fees (although goods are shipped to the customer's home). Nevertheless, customers can return anything bought online or from the catalog to any of 600 local stores, saving the cost of return postage. And the Web site has a store locator to make it easier.

Of course, Eddie Bauer's online sales must collect sales tax. Would they be better off separating the offline and online stores? Sure, they would avoid having to collect sales tax; but they'd lose cross-promotion, easy returns and the unified brand.

Some businesses can only exist on the Net. Examples are Talk City that offers chat services and Tripod (now part of Lycos) that offers free Web pages. Some will never do their business on the Net, such as barbershops and gas stations (although Priceline recently offered name-your-own-price gasoline sales when gas prices went up). A very few will clobber offline businesses, either replacing them completely or greatly diminishing them. Will newspapers eventually succumb to the Net? There seem to be few advantages to mail order catalog sales over online catalogs, except that not everyone is online yet. Most businesses, however, will see the Net as another channel to market.

When Internet businesses like Amazon and CDNow first appeared, some observers suspected that offline book and CD stores were in trouble. It is now becoming clear that, while online stores are important, they are not likely to replace physical stores.

Stores established in the physical world have huge advantages over Internet businesses. Many have strong established and trusted brands, distribution systems, local service and support. The challenge is to integrate existing physical stores with their online incarnations.

Office Depot (http://www.officedepot.com) is an outstanding example of online and offline integration. They have over 700 stores nationwide, catalog sales, and now a Web store. Shipping is free for orders over $50, eliminating one barrier to online sales. If the customer prefers, items ordered online can usually be picked up at a local store (no shipping charge) within four hours. Items bought in any of the stores or online can be returned to any store, a big advantage

over online-only stores that require items to be shipped back, usually at the customer's expense. Online customers can also maintain
shopping lists of frequently purchased items to make reorders easier.
And the online store isn't limited by store inventories: special order
items include three times the product numbers as those found in a
typical store.

Office Depot has shown how offline and online stores can be tightly
integrated to the benefit of the entire enterprise. Couple this with
the fact that established businesses typically have far more cash
available to build their online presence than Internet companies have
to build their offline infrastructure. The result is clear: Internet-only
businesses will be uncommon. Established offline businesses adding
an online component will be pervasive.

Most PC manufacturers sell through distributors, so to start selling
direct over the Net is to raise the ire of the distributors. PCOrder's
(http://www.pcorder.com) CommerceStation helps. Manufacturers can
use CommerceStation to enable customers to shop, select and con-
figure the systems they want, but then the order is passed to the
customer's local distributor. This way, PC manufacturers hope to stop
losing sales to the convenience of online custom PC orders provided
by the likes of Dell and Gateway.

Product Information

Commerce on the Net really shines for considered purchases. One
can present more information on more products and more ways to
compare product features and reviews than would be practical offline.
Information for car buyers at sites like AutobyTel.com is changing

the car buying experience. Do research and make a choice, then collect firm bids from local dealers. Go in and pick up your new car, no haggle, no hassle. AutoByTel.com has created a business based on referral fees and providing customers with all the information they are likely to need to make a car buying decision.

We normally think of product information as being fairly static. Here are our products, here are their benefits, here's what they cost. But the goal of presenting product information is to enable customers to see your products in their lives or businesses. Interaction engages the brain. Sometimes it even engages the imagination. It can go much farther than static description toward getting customers involved with the idea of using your products.

The Barbie site (http://www.barbie.com) allows visitors to design their own Barbie. Select skin color, eye color, hair color, outfit, accessories, name, home, hobbies, then order her. It's a product that the customer has been involved in creating, so likely more meaningful.

One of the best ways to generate interest in your products is to get potential customers involved with them. Touch them, hold them, if selling face to face. But if selling over the Net, interact with them.

The Room Planner at the Herman Miller store (http://www.hmstore.com) does exactly that. It's similar to the garden planner at Garden.com. Prospects can arrange furniture templates on a room diagram, then buy the furniture that they've just used to design the room.

Herman Miller has taken a smart next step. They also provide a paper version of the Room Planner to download and print. Finally, there is also a human room planner ready to help. Getting customers more involved with products can improve sales.

Land Rover helps customers to see exactly what they'd like to buy. The Land Rover site (http://best4x4.landrover.com) does this by an interactive feature called Outfit Your Land Rover. A Java applet enables the visitor to select his choice of color, mud flaps, brush guards, roof rack, wheels and running boards. Click and the color changes. Click and it has brush bars. (It would be nice to have the price updated as features are added or removed, but maybe they want us to play with it before we see the bad news.) Not only does the feature improve customer visualization of Land Rovers, but the interactivity gets her more involved with the Web site and the product.

There is a story about a toy from the 1980s called Transformers that sold poorly. They were clever toys. They looked like one thing, like a car, but through a series of manipulations they could be turned into something else, usually a robot-like character. There was very little interest from the kids until stories were created around the Transformers. A visitor to the Web site today (http://www.transformers.com) is immediately pulled into the fantasy of Transformers with,

Their ancestors waged war across the galaxy.

The conflict continues as two opposing factions
renew their struggle for control of the universe.

Once again, on a new battleground,
"The Beast Wars" have begun...

The stories created a framework the kids could use to play with the toys, and sales took off. The same sort of thing happens when those kids grow up.

One of the problems of bringing out new technology components is getting design engineers to understand how the components might be designed into their products. Texas Instruments (http://www.ti.com) recently redesigned their Semiconductor Products Web site with the express purpose of making application information more accessible for design engineers. TI's flagship products are DSPs (digital signal processors), products with broad potential (like other computer processors) but which require a lot of technical expertise to use. The idea of the site redesign was to collect as much product application information as possible and make it easy to find. The easier it is to envision applications of DSPs, the more likely design engineers will design them in, so the more TI could sell. The Web, being an excellent medium for making information of this sort available, was the obvious place to present the applications information. Through its site redesign and stronger focus on applications information, TI is differentiating its DSPs on the basis of product information.

Promotion

Self-promoting content

The dream of many Web site entrepreneurs is that their sites will promote themselves. The content on some sites is so compelling that it will draw lots of visitors. Certainly the search engines draw huge crowds of visitors, as do chat, news, weather, sports and stock market data. Free resources such as free Web space at Geocities, free e-mail at Hotmail and free calendars at When.com draw crowds of visitors, too. As the broadest categories of crowd-drawing, self-promoting content become dominated by market leaders, smaller, more targeted self-promoting sites have appeared.

Web Site Garage demonstrates that a good online service can draw a crowd. The Web Site Garage (http://www.websitegarage.com) will scan a Web page for spelling errors, HTML errors, assess the graphics, look for dead links and generally give you an idea of how well the page was executed. It's a great way to promote the services they sell: analysis of an entire site and consulting on how to improve a site.

Toshiba could have just made another corporate site talking about their line of copiers. Instead, they've sponsored a site of useful information and services for the people who would use their copiers: OfficeManager.com (http://www.officemanager.com). The site is organized like an office building. In the lobby visitors can buy flowers and gifts. In Human Resources, book travel, find health and family info, employment opportunities and business services. Goof off in the break room with recipes, games, psychics and the like. The Mail Room offers links to shipping companies, electronic postcards, search engines and office supplies catalog sites. Finally, there's a copier game in the Copy Center, but this office is mainly business: descriptions of Toshiba products.

The problem with using content to attract traffic to a Web site is, well, you have to have content! Fresh content. All the time. That's a lot of work, which makes it less attractive, particularly if the content isn't your main line of business. Games can solve that problem. Playing a game like Jeopardy! (http://www.station.sony.com/jeopardy/) can be a fresh experience each time it's played, so visitors may come back repeatedly.

Events have the power to draw a crowd. One of the most popular kinds of events for self-promotion on the Net is the scheduled chat session. Barnes and Noble (http://www.barnesandnoble.com) schedules an Author Chat every day. Each one draws hundreds and sometimes thousands of visitors. Visitors are drawn to the feeling of "being there." They are also attracted by the notion of being able to ask questions, in spite of the fact that only a handful of questions from a thousand visitors can be answered in an hour.

One of the most popular individual events on the Net has been the chess match in which Deep Blue defeated Garry Kasparov. Over 74 million hits to the IBM site (http://www.chess.ibm.com) were generated during the nine day event by over four million individuals. They not only saw the details of the games, but IBM had created an opportunity to show off its technical expertise.

There are many Web site self-promotion success stories. However, the vast majority of Web sites are not effectively self-promoting. They need help. Companies frequently make the mistake of assuming that having a Web site is sufficient promotion. If you build it, will they come? In most cases, no. If you build it, your pages will be among the half billion other pages out there. Effective promotion often differentiates successful online businesses from the rest.

E-mail promotion

Nobody likes spam, unsolicited commercial e-mail. On the other hand, newsletters and product announcements sent by e-mail is one of the most cost-effective ways for companies to promote themselves to customers. The difference is that newsletters, when done properly, are *solicited* commercial e-mail.

Companies like Postmaster Direct (http://www.postmasterdirect.com) build upon two ideas: the cost-effectiveness of e-mail advertising and the fact that when a potential buyer is interested in, say, tires, tire ads can be pretty darn fascinating!

Opt-in e-mail advertising collects e-mail addresses of buyers who want to receive ads in certain categories. These buyers have not just bought something else and unwittingly ended up on a mailing list, as is common in the offline direct marketing business. Rather, they have clicked on a checkbox asking to be sent e-mail ads. They are interested prospects. That's why e-mail ad campaigns to opt-in lists are uncommonly high: typically 5-15% response rates.

Opt-in is based on three principles:

- Notice: Full disclosure of what data is being collected about the list member and how it will be used.

- Choice: Members must opt-in to join and may opt-out any-time they wish.

- Access: Members can check, modify or delete their records at any time..

Links and affiliate programs

Promotion on the Web is about getting links to the promoted site. Differentiation by promotion is about getting more links than the competition. The most effective way to induce people to link to a site is through affiliate programs that pay a fee for referred purchases.

Setting up an affiliate program requires integrating tracking software with a shopping cart, locating affiliates, then managing the click-throughs, sales and payments. Affiliate program service bureaus can be a big help in signing up affiliates and handling the accounting. Merchants pay for that service, of course, so many prefer to implement their own affiliate programs. Several software packages are available for modest cost ($500-$700). A list of affiliate software packages is available at 2-Tier (http://www.2-tier.com/page.cfm/3365).

Perhaps the easiest way to start an affiliate program is through a service bureau. ClickTrade (http://www.clicktrade.com) is one of the most painless to work with, particularly for small businesses, because they charge no start-up fees (although there is a deposit toward future payments). Sites can choose among payment options: paying for click-throughs, sales leads or sales. ClickTrade helps recruit the affiliates and handles the tracking and payments.

LinkShare (http://www.linkshare.com) is another service that manages affiliate programs for e-commerce sites and has an impressive array of clients. Borders, Readers Digest, Disney, JCPenney, Dell, 1-800-Flowers, Virtual Vinyards, Sharper Image, Avon, Office Max, K-Tel, CBS Sportsline, ESPN Store and about 200 others. Why are

these companies willing to pay the $5000 start-up fee? LinkShare
offers several unusual benefits to online stores.

- LinkShare offers affiliate and conventional advertising program hybrids. For example, an Internet merchant can pay
  any affiliate (referring site) per thousand advertising impressions (CPM), per click-through, or based on a variable
  percent of the sale.

- LinkShare permits merchants to specify "return days," making it possible to compensate affiliates even when a referred customer returns directly to a merchant at a later
  date (bypassing the affiliate).

- LinkShare allows merchants to dynamically update campaign images and products without requiring changes on
  the affiliate site.

- LinkShare allows merchants to pay affiliates either in cash
  or store credits.

Effective ads

The most common form of online advertising, even if not the most
effective, is banner ads. Banner ads are links. The idea of placing
banner ads is that it is a way to create links to a site, but instead of
asking for the links, they are paid for. They generally conform to
standard sizes and page placements and, as a result, Web surfers
often simply tune them out. In many cases it is more effective, for

example, to pay for a block of text with a link on it than pay for a banner ad. If it doesn't look like an ad, it may not be ignored.

As with any advertising, the effectiveness of a banner ad campaign can be improved by careful selection of the target audience and design of the ad. John Hancock Insurance (http://www.hancock.com) used a banner ad that generated 10 times the click-through rate of typical Web ads. It's a form that says, "I'm __ years old and I make __ per year. What will I need to retire?" Simple. It is a common question and difficult to answer. And it's interactive. Of course, once it generates the answer it makes Hancock's array of products and services available to you to get started achieving the retirement goal.

Less common than banner ads, but very effective, is the sponsorship of a popular site. IBM has been the official Web site sponsor for the Olympics since the 1994 Winter Games in Norway. Being an official sponsor instead of just an advertiser sets the sponsor apart from other advertisers. Sponsorship is an enduring relationship where an ad is momentary. In the case of IBM's Web sponsorship, it is also a way to exercise and demonstrate capability. The Olympics get a huge number of hits. IBM has used the events (http://www.sydney.olympic.org) as a way to test and tune their capabilities in providing service to high volume sites. At the same time, they demonstrate that capability to millions of Web surfers.

Brand

The most common value proposition for subscription sites is quality. The notion of quality is usually expressed through brand recognition. I pay the subscription fee for the online version of *Business Week* (http://www.businessweek.com). I know the kind of information I'll find there, and I'm comfortable with the level of quality. In addition, I know that most executives read *Business Week*, so before I present to them I want to know what they've been exposed to. And the reason I subscribe to the Web site but not the paper magazine: I hate having all those magazines piling up around the house!

The *Wall Street Journal* (http://www.wsj.com) is the paper of record for the U.S. business community. In conjunction with its parent company, Dow Jones, it generates much of its own financial news. Because of its unique position in the market, many industry analysts give the Wall Street Journal a better chance than most to be able to make subscription work on the Web.

c|net (http://www.cnet.com) wants to be THE online source for information on technology products. They were doing well with a sold-out ad inventory but suffered from a low level of brand awareness. They had devoted visitors, but other Web users didn't know who they were. So a brand awareness campaign was created, the first step of which was to identify their perceived competition. ZDNet has a similar site, focused on information about computer technology with lots of articles, product comparisons and so forth. But c|net discovered that ZDNet was not seen as their primary competitor. They discovered that when people sought information on computers and other technology products, they either asked their friends or went directly to individual corporate Web sites of the product providers. Friends and companies were the competition, not ZDNet. So the branding campaign focused on the benefits of an authoritative, independent source of technology-product information, not the way c|net compares to ZDNet.

It is common in emerging markets to promote the idea of the new market and for the early participants in the market to be cooperative and supportive of one another. The important task at this stage is to establish the credibility and value of the new product category in the minds of potential customers. Later, after the market becomes better established, one would expect it to become more competitive for market share. At that point, direct comparisons (Coke vs. Pepsi) between leading competitors are more common.

Comfort

Customers must feel comfortable before they are willing to part with their money. IBM made a science of marketing FUD (Fear, Uncertainty and Doubt) when a technology manager had his job on the line and was considering a computer purchase from anyone other than the safe choice, IBM. We see vendors and services addressing FUD all over the Net today from browser vendors featuring encrypted transactions to services like TRUSTe and MasterCard Safe Site that will certify that a commerce site will handle your transaction and personal information responsibly. The irony of this approach is the vendor who sells on comfort often first creates anxiety about what *could* happen if the buyer doesn't make the right choice. Netscape, for example, stressed the value of its encrypted transactions, protecting against credit card thieves who could intercept credit card numbers as they zipped across the Net. The fact is, however, that credit card theft from card numbers moving across the Net never has been a problem. Credit card theft happens when hackers break into poorly secured databases containing thousands of credit card numbers—a problem that encrypted transactions does not address.

Comfort is part of the value of auto retail metamediary sites like AutobyTel.com. Few people enjoy the prospect of haggling for a car, especially when they are poorly informed. The automotive information at AutobyTel helps to reduce buyers' anxiety.

One of the most important characteristics of a brand is trust. Rather than the old saw that "familiarity breeds contempt," the fact is that familiarity breeds comfort. We return to trusted brands because we are comfortable with them. Even if we're unfamiliar with the products, we may choose a recognized brand on the assumption of quality and value as a comfortable choice. No doubt Amazon gets purchases from first time online buyers simply because they recognize the strong brand name.

Customer's Buying Reality

Installment buying was an innovation of the McCormick Reaper company, which recognized the difficulty farmers had in purchasing an expensive implement like a reaper. Lenox sold more fine china as gifts for new brides when it invented the bridal registry, which helped multiple gift givers to build a full china set one place setting at a time. These are examples of recognizing the limitations of the customer's buying reality, and overcoming them.

Nearly all consumer commerce on the Net is conducted through credit card transactions, but that leaves out a large segment of active consumers: teenagers. Few teens have credit cards, yet there are lots of teens surfing the Net. A few sites like ICanBuy.com have implemented schemes to create online accounts for teens from which they can purchase products without credit cards.

"Teen money management" sounds like an oxymoron, but that's what iCanBuy (http://www.icanbuy.com) is about. iCanBuy is an online savings club. Parents use their credit cards to deposit money in their kid's online savings account, held by Security First Network Bank. The kids can leave the money in the bank collecting interest or can spend it at the iCanBuy stores or can donate money to charity through the site. The scheme puts the teen in charge of managing his or her money while it gives the vendors on the iCanBuy site a way to sell without credit cards. Want something but don't have enough in the account? iCanBuy also provides a Wish List feature which teens can use to let friends and relatives know what they'd like. The kids have responsibility but parents still have control: They can review purchases and block them, if they wish.

Pricing Strategies

About a hundred years ago when a safety razor cost about a week's wages, Gillette devised one of the most famous and effective pricing strategies: sell the expensive razors at a loss, creating greater demand for blades, which were inexpensive but would have to be purchased again and again and again.

One of the most common pricing strategies used on the Net today is, give it away for free. Netscape gave its browser away for free, which cost Netscape very little. The pricing policy created demand for Netscape's server software, which they sold. The more free Netscape browsers people downloaded, the greater the demand for servers that supported secure transactions.

GeoCities (now Yahoo!Geocities) offers free Web sites. Hotmail and others offer free e-mail. Everybody offers free information and entertainment. And FreePC.com (http://www.freePC.com) offers a free PC. The Net has brought us into a time of information abundance. When information was relatively scarce, intermediaries like travel agents and brokers could even charge for it! No more. The Net has given so much information to so many, the new scarce resource is *attention*. Advertisers must go to greater lengths to get it, even if it means giving away lots of free stuff in exchange for the right to impose ads—in other words, in exchange for a sliver of your attention. The purpose of advertising is to generate sales of products and services, but these products and services are attractively priced (free!) to generate attention for advertising.

Networks are great at sharing information. Shared information implies common standards. An audio file, for example, cannot be shared and heard unless the people sharing it have compatible audio players. When incompatible products enter a market at the same time, the one that gets the most users is often the one that prevails. Rapid growth is essential to establishing a product as the platform of choice. So it is with streaming audio and video formats. Real (http://www.real.com) has moved aggressively in an attempt to become the standard platform for streaming media. Pricing strategy was critical: Give the players away for free until it becomes the standard platform.

Pricing strategy is behind one of the hottest movements in business-to-business buying. The pricing strategy: Don't set price. Let the marketplace decide. Auctions are becoming widely used as a way to determine efficient prices for goods and services. Companies like FreeMarkets (http://www.freemarkets.-com) and VerticalNet (http://www.verticalnet.com) set up auctions in vertical markets. The first online B2B auctions were for one-of-a-kind goods such as used industrial tools or production overruns. Increasingly, auctions are moving into the bidding process for component parts or business services. Online auctions open the bidding to more buyers and more sellers, creating more dynamic pricing.

Referrals

News travels fast on the Net, so it is a rich medium for referrals. And since referrals are among the least expensive and most effective marketing methods, companies can strongly differentiate themselves if they can generate large numbers of referrals. One of the most powerful referral programs on the Net, now widely duplicated, is affiliates, pioneered by Amazon.com. If anyone puts an affiliate link to an Amazon product on his own Web site, and if a customer clicks on that link and makes the purchase, Amazon pays a referral fee of 5-15%. Affiliate programs have been enormously successful. Amazon alone boasts nearly half a million affiliates and there are thousands of other affiliate programs available across the Web.

Some online stores operate exclusively on referrals. Computers.com (http://www.computers.com) lists lots of information about 120,000 products from 85 manufacturers. It makes computer comparison-shopping easy. But Computers.com doesn't actually sell computers them-selves. Instead, revenues come from two sources: ads and commis-sions. One of the features of Computers.com is to pull current prices on products from many online retailers, then present them all in a neat table to the visitor. The visitor decides where to buy, clicks to go to that online store, and if he buys, Computers.com gets a refer-ral fee.

Personal networking is another name for referrals. The notion is that there are at most six degrees of separation between any two people. A knows B (one degree of separation), B knows C, C knows D and D knows E. There are four degrees of separation between A and E. Much of the world works on contacts. Can the Net facilitate making connections? The idea behind the SixDegrees Web site (http:/ /www.sixdegrees.com) is exactly that. By registering on the site and entering your friends and relatives as contacts, you enter into a cloud of connections.

It's an interesting idea and maybe it will work for people. Whether it does or not, there's a lesson to be learned. SixDegrees has assembled a huge membership list through referrals. When I register and enter a couple of friends' names as other possible members, they get e-mails that refer to me. They are likely to respond to messages about their friends. They may register, just as I did, simply to find out what this thing is. Referrals beget referrals, and the process continues.

One of the most effective forms of promotion is word of mouth re-ferrals. How can it be encouraged on the Net? Many online publica-tions do what TechWeb (http://www.techweb.com) has done. Each ar-ticle includes a "Send as e-mail" button, which allows the visitor to send the article he's viewing to a friend. Word of mouth becomes word of e-mail and the button not only makes it easy but also prompts the visitor to think about whom else might be interested in this site. Want to make it even easier? Save e-mail addresses in a cookie and show them as a list to choose from.

Recommend-It (http://www.recommend-it.com) is another mechamism to spread word-of-mouth referrals. Here's how it works: you put a Recommend-It button on your site inviting customers to click it if they like what they see. They have an opportunity to send recommendation e-mails to as many as three people. Also, Recommend-It counts the recommendations and publishes the results in its free newsletter.

E-mail is a convenient medium for referral, but links are better. Links are more permanent. Netscape and Microsoft induced millions of Web site builders to include a "referral" link on their sites stating that this site is best viewed by a certain browser. More typical link equity is Web page builders voluntarily creating links to a site. We will discuss link equity more later in the book.

Repeat Business

Repeat business tends to be very economical due to low marketing costs. Companies can differentiate themselves by developing effective programs to generate repeat business. One of the most attractive mechanisms is e-mail since it costs nothing to send and it goes to the customer rather than waiting for the customer to take the initiative. Cassette House, an online vendor of blank cassettes and other audio gear, motivates mailing list members to read the newsletters by offering fabulous sales only to newsletter subscribers. Customers come for the sale items but usually leave buying other items as well. Cassette House generates repeat business with its newsletters and is able to offer customers bargains on overstocked products.

Certain kinds of information lend themselves to repeat visits. It's the idea behind news, weather and sports. One must check back regularly to keep informed. Maxwell Technologies (http:// traffic.maxwell.com) offers real time traffic maps for selected cities. Major roads are color coded by traffic speed. There are also reports on traffic incidents, construction closures and the weather. There's great advertising potiential in a site that solves a problem that lots of people have, especially a problem like this one that is faced at least a couple of times each day.

Some sites create their own news. Online polls and surveys like those at Motley Fool (http://www.fool.com/PollingAllFools/PollingAllFools.asp) are perhaps the easiest way to give visitors a voice in a site. Click, click, click and an opinion is registered. It's also an easy way for them to see what their fellow visitors are thinking. With interesting questions, site visitors are curious to see the results, which may draw them back for repeat visits. Polls can be done on nearly any subject so they can be employed at nearly any Web site. Be careful, however, about believing the results. Since there are generally no controls on who is taking the poll or how many times they've voted, results should be viewed more as entertainment than information.

Quizzes and calculators like those at the Mayo Clinic's site (http://www.mayohealth.org/mayo/library/htm/quiz.htm) lie somewhere between fresh content and reference work. They're easy to implement and they can be adapted to any subject area. That means that whatever kind of information your Web site offers, there's a good chance it could be enhanced with some quizzes and calculators. A health and fitness site, for example, may bring visitors back to repeatedly calculate their body mass index.

Horsenet (http://www.horsenet.com) offers everything you ever wanted to know about horses. It's most importantly a community for horse people. It makes money through banner ads, building and hosting other horse-related sites, offering Horsenet e-mail addresses, hosting chat events and selling over 2,000 products.

Newspapers see news stories as content and classified ads as one of the main revenue generators. Horsenet offers classified ads but unlike the newspaper business model, the classifieds are free. The ad posting process is completely automated. Costs are virtually nonexistent. And the classified ads pull in a lot of traffic and repeat visits. It's one of the most popular areas of the Horsenet site.

Most sites that exist to sell ads attract their audience with content. Visto (http://www.visto.com) attracts its audience with resources that also ensure that their visitors return. Visto offers free file space (up to 15 MB), an address book, free e-mail, an online calendar, a to-do list tracker and a bookmark manager. Visitors who maintain this information on the Net can then access it from anywhere with any computer.

The cost of these resources is paid in two ways: Users are exposed to ads (and demographic information is collected when they subscribe) and users are charged if they exceed the 15MB limit. Bits are cheap, attention is valuable, and people will come back to see their own stuff.

Excite offers anyone the ability to build a community discussion area at no charge (http://www.excite.com/communities/directory/). The creator controls access to the community. When someone requests to join a community, an e-mail is sent to the creator, who decides who gets in and who doesn't. Excite Communities offers

- Discussions: Build a forum for discussing hot topics.

- Calendar: Mark the calendar with community events.

- Bookmarks: List Web sites of interest to your community.

- Contact List: Share contact info with members of your community.

- Photos: Share photo albums and favorite snapshots.

- Chat: Chat with fellow members in the community's private chat room.

The business objective in providing this extensive free service: Build repeat traffic and sell advertising to individually identified participants (ZIP code, birth date and gender requested upon registration).

14 Universal Differentiators

---

*Things are constantly changing and that means
you constantly have to test. The key for us is
learning. We constantly try new things...what
we don't want to do is make the same mistake
twice. I want to get that culture in place: that
it's okay to try something, make a mistake,
that's part of the game, and learn quicker...that's
one of the things that's helped us get our
leadership position...because we've tried three
things and now we know which one works.*

— Jamie O'Neill, COO, Garden.com

Two differentiation strategies are open to every market: Be the low
cost leader and learn faster than your competitors.

Low Cost

Companies differentiate themselves by becoming the low cost provider for the industry. The low cost provider must attend to cutting
costs in every function of its organization, but do so without compro-

mising product features or quality. It's a common strategy since every manager knows that low cost differentiation is an option open to him. Differentiation along other dimensions typically requires more creative thought. The economics of the Net encourages some forms of low cost strategy, such as NetMarket's approach to retail: Offer everything, stock nothing, pass orders on to manufacturers for fulfillment.

The low cost provider is the one that costs the customer the least. One generally thinks in terms of lowest purchase price, but a large price factor is often the cost of making the product useful once it arrives. Apple Macintosh computers were differentiated from PCs by ease of use. In fact, customers were willing to pay a premium purchase price for the time and frustration savings generated by the Mac's ease of use.

Learning Faster

Like cost, learning is a factor that cuts through all aspects of a company. It's important in all businesses but particularly important in businesses in the midst of tumultuous markets, stirred by rapidly developing technology and innovative business models. Perhaps the advantages of fast learning can be best appreciated when looking at companies of the opposite stripe: companies that stifle innovation, that refuse to experiment, that look inward rather than outward and that fail to appreciate the opportunities hidden in unexpected successes and failures.

How does an online store learn the right inventory to carry? Chuck Moss, founder of Discount Games (http://www.discountgames.com), spends at least an hour a day reading the gaming newsgroups. He learns what people are saying about his company and his competitors. He also quickly learns what people are looking for but can't find, and adds it to his inventory.

Most businesses ignore discussion groups. Certainly, many discussion groups are a total waste of time, but many aren't. Many companies have the opportunity for direct daily contact with their marketplace through discussions. For customers who want to know their customers, it's an opportunity that shouldn't be missed.

Companies that offer customized products have a learning opportunity with each order. What are the current customer preferences? Check which options were ordered today. Dell and Gateway discover in real time what customers are looking for now. Businesses that buy and sell their parts in auctions and online exchanges get real time feedback about the rising and falling value of their offerings. Online magazine publishers who measure traffic to individual articles get immediate feedback on what interests readers most and what interests them least. What article titles are the most enticing?

Business on the Net offers unprecedented opportunities for experimentation and measurement. Those companies that use the opportunities to learn quickest are in the best position to use the advantage of learning to build other competitive advantages.

15 How to Choose?

*Curly (Jack Palance character): You know what
        the secret to life is?*
Mitch (Billy Crystal character): No, what?
Curly: This.
Mitch: Your finger?
*Curly: One thing. Just one thing. You stick to
        that and everything else don't mean shit.*
Mitch: That's great but...what's the one thing?
Curly: That's what you've got to figure out.

— from the movie *City Slickers*

How does management choose the right differentiation strategies?
A company must focus on one or a combination of a few to get the
greatest impact. One of the biggest threats to business in general
and online business specifically is the amount of available opportunity. Go for it all and you will go nowhere. Find your one thing and
you have a chance.

- Will the difference make a difference to the customers?
  Will the added cost of differentiating your offering be more
  than offset by higher profits?

- Is the differentiation sustainable; or, if successful, can competitors readily copy it, wiping out your uniqueness?

Making a Difference to Customers

A product or service must be different in order to be better, but not all differences are improvements. The important criterion is, will *customers* value the difference? If not, the difference is not a matter of competitive strategy.

Differences can be viewed in two ways: the actual differences in product features and specifications and the differences perceived by customers. A common mistake is to differentiate products without effectively communicating the differences to customers. If the customer doesn't see a difference, it hardly matters whether it's there or not. Customers are unlikely to pay a premium for differences that they don't know about.

Customers do pay for appealing differences that they perceive. Perceived differences may increase demand without actual product differences. A classic example is how sales for Perrier bottled water increased when the price was increased. No change in the product, just an increase in price. But the higher price translated to a perception of a higher quality product, and sales went up.

When creating product differences, companies must find a way to communicate the differences and the benefits of the differences to customers. This can be increasingly difficult as products get more complex, less understandable to typical consumers, so it must be translated from the language of product features to the language of customer benefits. If customers cannot understand the benefits, the company would do well to reconsider the value of the difference.

Differences That Pay

The ultimate test for whether a product or service difference makes a difference to customers is: will they pay for it? Does the difference generate either higher profits or increased sales? It generally costs money to differentiate products, so the effort is justified only if the increased costs generate increased returns. I am fully aware that I probably end up paying more cash to buy books online, but the convenience is substantial and my time is worth something. Further, I realize I could do all my book shopping at Books.com which shows a price comparison with other online retailers and proves that their prices are lower, but I shop at Amazon for the differences: 1-Click Ordering, customer reviews, book recommendations and the comfort of the familiar. These are differences I am willing to pay for.

Another view is whether customers are compelled to use your product. Let's say that you have an exclusive agreement to broadcast a corporate stockholders meeting over the Net. Assuming there are people who really must see the broadcast, they are compelled to be your customer. They have no alternative.

It may sound a bit old-fashioned in the days of wild Internet stock valuations, but the business must be designed to be profitable. Differentiation that will not lead to higher profits is a waste of effort.

Those profits may be delayed but that must be the motivation, that must be the end result.

Sustainable Differences

Once a difference is created for which customers are willing to pay, the competition will notice. What will they do? Can they readily copy your difference and wipe out your advantage? If they do copy your difference, will the difference have created a new subcategory in which you are the leader? If so, even if your difference is copied, you may retain the leadership advantage in the minds of customers.

Differentiation based on inventions can be sustained through patent protection or guarding the invention as a trade secret. By getting a patent on its reverse auction business model, Priceline.com has a sustainable difference from the other online travel sites.

Differentiation can be sustained by contract. NetMarket sells products from many manufacturers who fulfill orders by shipping purchases directly to customers. It's a sustainable difference if NetMarket has stipulated in their contracts with manufacturers that they will be the sole Internet representative of the manufacturer's products.

Some differences can be copied without diminishing their value for the innovator. For example, Amazon.com collects information on customer preferences and buying behavior to use when recommending books. BarnesandNoble.com has implemented a similar system. But the existence of the BarnesandNoble.com database does not substantially diminish the value of the database at Amazon. Amazon still knows all those customers and their behavior. If a longtime

Amazon customer were to visit BarnesandNoble, they wouldn't have the relationship history and accumulated information that exists at Amazon. Assuming that history yields better recommendations, it's the history that would draw customers back, not the existence of the system itself.

Sometimes competitors are slow to respond to innovations. The longer a competitor waits to respond to a differentiation strategy, the stronger impression the differentiator can make in the minds of customers. There are several reasons why a threatened competitor may be slow to respond.

Competitors simply might not be paying attention. This often happens, but it must not become the basis of a differentiation strategy. The strategy of hoping for inattention is no strategy at all. When competitors are napping, it may be lucky for the differentiating company, but do not plan on it.

Competitors may be unable to respond. If a company has suffered financial hardships, has had turmoil in its key personnel or is being attacked on many fronts by different attackers possibly in different markets, they may be distracted or unable to respond to yet another threat from a differentiation strategy.

Perhaps the most attractive situation, however, is when a competitor will not want to respond. This is often referred to as competitive judo.

Judo seeks to use the opponent's strengths to one's own advantage, rather than to oppose it directly. Competitive judo is the strategy of using the competitor's momentum against him. For example, when tiny Netscape competed with giant Microsoft in the browser market, Microsoft seemed to have tremendous advantages. It had influence over nearly every computer manufacturer because it monopolized the operating system market. But Netscape recognized that this strength could be used against Microsoft. Microsoft preferred to build the best browser for its own operating systems. So Netscape offered browsers for many operating systems in addition to Windows, including Macintosh and many versions of Unix. It helped Netscape to become recognized as the open standard browser. Netscape soon had over 80% of the installed base of browsers. Their position was secure enough to start charging for browsers, which had previously been given away. Soon, browser sales provided the main portion of Netscape's revenues. Now it was Microsoft's turn for competitive judo. Microsoft gave their browser away for free and started to take market share away from Netscape. Netscape was slow to respond—browser sales were their main revenue source. By the time Netscape did return to free browser downloads two years later, Netscape had lost its market share advantage.

Dell versus Compaq is another example of competitive judo. By the time Dell started selling computers in volume in the mid-1980s, Compaq and other manufacturers had a considerable advantage in retail distribution. They had locked up the limited shelf space in computer stores and had strong alliances with channel partners. Rather than oppose those strengths, Dell pursued a direct distribution model that turned out to have a number of advantages over retail distribution, such as the elimination of finished goods inventory. Recognizing these advantages, Compaq attempted to follow suit in 1998 and 1999 but had difficulties due to channel conflicts. Retailers did not want Compaq disintermediating them by selling direct. Compaq's retail channel strength had become a liability, giving Dell more time to build on the advantages of selling direct.

16 Brand Building: Keep It In Mind

What is the single most important objective of the marketing process? What is the glue that holds the broad range of marketing functions together?

We believe it is the process of branding.

Marketing is building a brand in the mind of the prospect.

— Al Ries and Laura Ries,
The 22 Immutable Laws of Branding

One Concept

Building a brand is the process of reserving space in the minds of customers for a product and a company. How does one induce millions of people to learn anything, particularly learn about your company and your product? First, keep it simple. Focus on one concept for customers to know. Garden.com has a nice, simple proposition, an online gardening superstore. eBay has online auctions; Dell has computers built to order; BarnesandNoble.com has millions of books. CDNOW has online CD superstore

Some online businesses, after their first successes, have increased the breadth of their offerings, thereby muddling their brand. Amazon.com, for example, had a widely recognized and understood brand as the world's biggest bookstore. Their aspirations were grander than books, however. They now sell CDs, video, computers, electronics, software, toys, auctions, art and collectibles, tools and hardware, and lawn and patio products. It has become much more difficult to describe Amazon's business. It may be very general, like "online retailer," but that is too general to be of much use. They now use the tag line "The Earth's Biggest Selection." They may be moving to a simpler concept, but during this transition period they have generated some confusion.

The search engines have also generated some confusion by expanding their breadth to become "portals." Ask a Net user what a search engine is and you'll get a cogent answer. Ask what a portal is and, at best, you're likely to get an answer like "a search engine and other stuff." Like Amazon, the portals currently appear to many to be a collection of businesses under one name. Each business may generate a lot of traffic, but the businesses of the portals don't have an obvious theme to bind them together. Yahoo! seems like "reference information" with its Web directory, phone numbers, and maps. That's broadened to "news and reference" with its news, sports, weather, TV listings and stock quotes and the MyYahoo! page that customizes the news. But where do free e-mail, chat rooms, games, classified ads, personal ads, auctions, shopping, build-your-own-store and build-your-own-Website fit? From Yahoo!'s point of view, these are all businesses from which they can derive ad revenues. The view to a typical Net surfer is incoherent. However, Yahoo!'s customer, the one who puts down the money, is the advertiser. To the advertiser, Yahoo! is a provider of a huge volume of online ad exposures. But to continue to grow those ad revenues, increasing numbers of Net surfers have to come to Yahoo! For that to happen, they need a simple association in their minds between Yahoo! and what they can expect to get there.

Own a Word

Reserve an association in customers' minds between your business and a concept. Keep it simple. The ultimate in simplicity is when the concept is a word. Auction? eBay. Books? Amazon. Directory? Yahoo! Router? Cisco. Browser? Netscape used to own this one. Now they share it with Microsoft. Reverse auction? Priceline owns it, but it's not exactly a household word.

How does a company come to own a word? The first step is to dominate a market nearly to the point of monopoly. Easier said than done, of course, but one key is to be the first into the market. Not only is there a first mover advantage to gaining market share, there is a first mover advantage for mind share. In some cases the company name will become a generic word for the category. Lots of competitors have moved into the copier business, but we still say, "I'll make you a xerox," even when using a Canon copier. We fedex packages when using Airborne's overnight service and go out for a coke in spite of the fact that we may be drinking Pepsis.

In addition to being first, keep every communication consistent with the association between the word and the company. This isn't often done in practice. As I write this, Cisco is running ads not about routers, but about the Internet. I doubt that Cisco or anyone else will ever own the word "Internet." Priceline.com does a good job of hammering home the idea of "you name your own price" in its ads, and Pets.com is consistent with its pet stuff concept in its sock puppet ads.

The benefit of a strong association with a concept and owning a word is that when a customer thinks of that concept or work, the associated company comes to mind. Once the prospect is thinking about a company, the selling can begin.

Easy to Find

A friend of mine, Steve Martin (not the actor) runs the Widescreen Movie Center (http://www.cheezmo.com/wsmc). He mentioned the other day that a surprisingly large percentage of his visitors come from Yahoo! and the search engines. A few searches quickly showed why. The site shows up on the first page of search results for "widescreen" on every search utility I checked: Yahoo!, Excite, AltaVista, Lycos, Infoseek and Hotbot.

I recently served on a panel discussion about Internet business success stories with Rebecca Anderson of SEA Medical Services (http://rampages.onramp.net-/~seamed). She and others were telling their success stories. Rebecca's Web site produced nothing at first but suddenly became busy and nearly doubled her revenues (previously, all offline). Take a look at the site. It violates nearly every rule you can think of: not fancy, can't buy online, not registered with search engines, no meta tags. But it generates business effectively! Why?

The key is that she was one of the first and is still one of the few business Web sites in her market, alcohol breath analysis tools. Once the search engine spiders found and indexed her site, it began showing up high on market-specific searches.

People get to a Web site in one of three ways. They type in a URL, follow a link, or use a search engine (a special case of following a link). Many experts stress the importance of search engine placement as a primary form of online promotion. Good search engine placement (first or second page of search results for an important keyword) can bring a lot of traffic to a site, but the obvious fact is that it's rare. Assume there are a million Web sites and everyone wants to be in the top 20 links from search engines. That would mean that 50,000 keywords would have to return completely different sets of results to please the owners of a million sites. But typically people only use a vocabulary of about 5,000 words, so it's not going to happen.

Consider a few examples. Do any of these companies appear in the top 20 search engine hits for the corresponding keywords? Microsoft: software, operating system? Oracle: database? Xerox: copier? General Motors: automobile, car? IBM, HP or Compaq: computer? Kenmore, Sears, Whirlpool: refrigerator? Scotts: fertilizer? Hershey, Mars: chocolate? Nike, Adidas, New Balance, Saucony: running shoes? Barnes and Noble, Borders, Amazon: books? Casio, HP, Texas Instruments: calculator? Checking Altavista, the answer is no. These companies are strongly associated with their corresponding keywords in public consciousness, but that doesn't necessarily mean a good search engine ranking. If companies' Web sites are to be found on the Net, they must usually be found through some means other than search engines.

The first alternative to search engines is directory sites. Directories like Yahoo! are commonly confused with search engines but they work differently and serve a different purpose. Directory sites index Web sites where other search engines index Web pages. It is imperative that a company gets its site listed at Yahoo! and other market-specific directories. On a directory your company has a better chance of being found when a Net surfer has a company name or product category in mind.

The second alternative to search engines is simply typing in a URL. For that to happen, the URL must be memorable and the company behind it has to come to mind.

The third alternative to search engines is general links on miscellaneous Web pages.

In the following sections, we will discuss the keys to the two alternatives to search engines: getting people to type in a URL and issues of getting links to your site.

Domain Name

Owning a word in the minds of the general public is a tough thing to do. Companies have a lot more control over their choice of domain name. It should be chosen to be easy to remember and evocative of the company. The most obvious choice is the name of the company, such as IBM.com, Intel.com or Ford.com. Some are too generic.

Who is eat.com? Ragu, the spaghetti sauce people. Too generic. Some are too difficult to remember. The Altavista search engine used to be altavista.digital.com. Big improvement when it was changed to altavista.com. The Charles Schwab Web site used to be eSchwab.com. Schwab.com is much better. Southwest Airlines greatly improved its domain name to southwest.com. Only the most dedicated customer would have remembered the old name, iflyswa.com.

On most Web sites, the largest number of visitors arrives after typing a URL into their browser. In spite of all the attention that search engines get as a tool for online promotion, more Net surfers know where they want to go, type in the address and go there. That is why online companies must work for a place in the mind of their customers and prospects.

Buzz

It is important to have an association between a concept, word, domain name and a company in the mind of customers and prospects. But, important as that association is, it is better that the prospect actively think about the company and its products. That is the power of buzz—publicity that gets people thinking and talking about sites, companies and products.

There are some masters of buzz. eBay is one. It seems that a week doesn't go by without hearing some story about eBay. Not all of it is particularly good, like when there was controversy about human body parts being offered for sale on eBay. For the most part, we hear a lot of interesting stories about odd and quirky items for sale and the recreational aspects of the auctions.

Some sites and businesses are magnets for publicity. Unclaimed Baggage (http://www.unclaimedbaggage.com), a company in Alabama that sells the contents of all the airlines' luggage that has gone unclaimed, is frequently contacted by news media asking to do stories on the unusual business. Unclaimed Baggage does not actively seek publicity; it simply keeps coming to them. But they promote one thing: They always feature their URL in their publicity. And after every story on *Oprah* or the *Today Show* or in a newspaper, traffic and sales on the Web site spike.

It is often the case that the source of a company's differentiation is also the source of its publicity opportunities. If your differentiation is exclusive Internet broadcast rights to certain rock concerts and your next concert is the Rolling Stones, there is an opportunity for publicity. If your site auctions rare and unusual items and a 17th Century Jean Le Clerc masterpiece is offered on the site, there is an opportunity for publicity. If your differentiation is to be the most advanced online store and you have become the first to offer Internet shopping on wireless phones, there is an opportunity for publicity. Not only is the differentiation strategy the source of publicity, it is exactly how you would like the marketplace to be thinking about you.

Link Equity

Online publicity differs from offline publicity in two ways: It is more persistent and it provides a direct link to the site. *Oprah* did a show on the best-kept shopping secrets in America. It listed, among others, the Unclaimed Baggage Center. Oprah has millions of viewers, so the show generated lots of business for Unclaimed Baggage. Great for business. However, after a mention on television, the public memory quickly fades. Consider, however, being listed on a Web page of best-kept shopping secrets. The page would tend to persist over time, perhaps months or years. The reach of a popular show like *Oprah* is enormous, but the persistence of an online link is far greater.

Online publicity, instead of being focused on mentions in editorial content, is focused on adding to the collection of links to a site. The more links to a site there are scattered around the Net on relevant pages, the greater the chance that a site will generate traffic from interested surfers.

Several years ago, the best way to get powerful online publicity was to get listed on a site like Cool Site of the Day (http://www.coolsiteoftheday.com). That was in the days when coolness was the best thing going for a Web site.   It would be beneficial to have a site listed on a service like the Incredibly Useful Site of the Day (http://www.zdnet.com/yil/content/depts/useful/useful.html). Once mentioned, sites of the day go into the Useful Site Library. They continue to get traffic from that exposure well past their special day of fame.

With serious business happening on the Web, publicity comes from mentions and links on industry-relevant sites. A mention and link in a review article for a computer product in c|net or ZDNet can give a site a boost. VerticalNet (http://www.verticalnet.com) organizes

information about more than fifty vertical industries. Like an ongoing trade magazine/trade show/marketplace these vertical market
centers can generate traffic and business for companies within the
market with mentions and links within the editorial content.

One of the most successful strategies for building link equity was
used by both Netscape and Microsoft in the promotion of their browsers. Browser technology changed quickly and site designers were
eager to design to the latest browser features, allowing the designers to do more cool stuff on the site. Owners of old-technology
browsers could not see the more advanced features of the sites;
and, worse, sites would often not work at all when viewed with old
browsers. Netscape and Microsoft made buttons and links available
for site designers that said, "Best viewed with..." either Netscape
Navigator or Microsoft Internet Explorer. The links were installed on
millions of sites, creating millions of links back to the Netscape and
Microsoft sites, providing these two companies with enormous link
equity.

Perhaps the most successful widely used method of generating link
equity is affiliate programs. Amazon implemented affiliate programs
on the Net as a way to generate referrals for book sales. The idea is
that anyone can join the affiliate program, then list products for sale
on his site. For example, I am an Amazon affiliate through my Web
site. I list reviews of a number of recommended books on e-business. A site visitor can read a review, then click on a link to buy the
item, but the link is to the corresponding product page on Amazon's
site. If the customer completes the purchase at the Amazon site,
Amazon fulfills the order and sends a referral fee, typically 5-15%,
to the affiliate who listed the item—in this case, to me. Through the

affiliate program, Amazon has created a lot of link equity, but it's the best kind—it links directly to transactions.

Amazon currently has about 400,000 affiliates with links to its site numbering in the millions. Affiliate programs are an excellent way to build link equity for an online business and have been widely adopted. There are currently over 2,000 active affiliate programs on the Net.

Online store owners can readily add affiliate programs to their stores by working with an affiliate program service. Companies such as ClickTrade (http://www.clicktrade.com), LinkShare (http://www.linkshare.com) and Commission Junction (http://www.cj.com) offer an intermediary service. Affiliates add links to their sites that link to the intermediary. The intermediary then links to the store owner's site and keeps track of the traffic and transactions.

Authority

A Web site for margarine? You bet. And one for spaghetti sauce, one for popsicles, another for hair color, another for herb packets, and more. These are some of more than 50 branded Web sites by the consumer product giant Unilever. But no one is going to buy a box of Popsicles and have them fedexed, so what are these Web sites about? In a word, branding.

The I Can't Believe It's Not Butter Web site (http://www.tasteyoulove.com) carries their romance advertising theme online. It features a serialized romance novel in the form of a diary, tips on romance and love, romantic electronic postcards, advice from the online Love Guru and recipes for romantic meals. Why? The sites are designed to be entertaining, but only as a vehicle to position the brand as authoritative and to strengthen the emotional association with the brand. I Can't Believe It's Not Butter: Romance. Ragu sauce: Warm family feelings. Popsicles: Fun. The sites are also useful for disseminating product use tips, contests and trial offers, which are harder to do through TV ads. The Web sites offer the brands depth and persistence as opposed to TV ads, which are intrusive, and offer broad exposure.

Some sites offer authority as a means to a commercial end. AutobyTel, for example, offers all the information a car buyer would need to make an informed purchase decision. The end result of all that information is the transaction fee that AutobyTel collects when a visitor decides to buy a car through the site or buy insurance or financing.

There are thousands of medical information sites on the Web. Most of them earn their money by selling ad space, but the appeal to the Web site visitor, the thing that draws a crowd, is thorough and authoritative medical information. In the case of sites like DrKoop.com (http://www.drkoop.com), thousands of pages of medical information is intended to draw consumers to the site who can then be exposed to ads and who may sign up for HMOs or other services that DrKoop.com can generate transaction fees from. The first step is authoritative information that brings visitors to the site.

Promote the Category

In an emerging market, the biggest challenge generally does not come from competition. It comes from ignorance of and indifference toward the category altogether. Too often potential customers don't even know this kind of product exists. For example, c|net (http://www.cnet.com) did a study to determine where they stood in the online marketplace of information about computers and software. They were expecting their primary competition to be ZDNet (http://www.zdnet.com), which offers similar information. They found that potential visitors were not making a choice between c|net and ZDNet. Instead, most of their potential visitors did not even know that such sites about computer products existed. As a result, c|net targeted its advertising not to compare themselves with the competition, but to describe the benefits of gathering product information before purchase. In other words, they promoted the category.

Web rings are a commonly used technique to promote a collection of Web sites in a category. Several Web rings, for example, link Star Trek sites to one another. Web rings typically consist of a set of links installed on the home page of each site in the ring. The link set includes a link to the next site in the ring, the previous site and sometimes links to random sites in the ring or a complete listing of all sites in the ring.

Commercial sites are usually reluctant to link to their competition, but not always. Web rings are common among erotic Web sites, promoting the category. However one might feel about erotic content on the Net, it is certainly the case that these sites have been leading the way to profitability among online businesses.

A ticket is just the thing to sell over the Net. The customer doesn't have to see it or touch it to make up his mind. Most tickets are expensive enough to justify credit card purchase. And the transaction is primarily information-based: A good ticket vendor would be able to provide the customer with details of the event, seating arrangements at the venue and so on.

Tickets.com (http://www.tickets.com) goes a couple of steps beyond the basics. First, they offer a ticket auction for unsold tickets just prior to the event. Customers might get a good deal and it's a good deal for the ticket sellers: No one benefits from an empty seat at a rock concert or basketball game. The other extra step Tickets.com takes is to tell customers other places to buy the tickets—in other words, who the competition is! Bad idea? Maybe not. If Tickets.com has competitive prices and if they can get customers to think, "Go to tickets.com first, no matter where you get the tickets," it's likely to be good business.

Part IV
What's Next?

Prediction is always difficult but especially about the future.

— Neils Bohr

As I finish this book there have been some wild gyrations in the stock market. Many dot-com companies (some mentioned herein), have lost a great deal of their market capitalization. Others have been fairly stable through it all. What is coming next?

As was discussed in the beginning of the book, most of the online markets are in the emerging or growth phases. We can expect to see speculation and extravagant expectations (which we have) and we can expect to see shakeouts where businesses disappear through mergers, acquisitions and simply shutting their doors. This has apparently begun in some of the online markets. Painful as it might be (especially for those heavily invested in dot-coms), it is a predictable and nearly inevitable step in the process toward mature online markets.

What else can we expect? The strategic themes (New Economics, New Relationships, New Timing, Dissolution of Distance and Network Effects), the advantages of doing business online compared to offline, will be the foundation for continued dramatic growth in online business. Yet in spite of rapid growth in many online markets, the less able competitors will fall away. The profits of survivors will grow. The survivors will be the leaders and those with sustainable differentiation. Competition among the online businesses will be fierce, but any business that is not online will find the competition even tougher.

Stable, profitable online market leaders will emerge. Most will retain their profitable leadership positions for decades into the future. And they will be big. The total volume of business conducted online will grow from the economic sideshow that it is today to a major force in national and global economies. The leading brands will be national and global in scope because the Net is global in scope and because on the Net, there is no distance.

The enabling technologies of microelectronics and communications continue their ongoing revolutions. Computers will continue to get faster and have greater capacity just as Moore's Law dictates. Communication bandwidth will continue to increase. The effect will be online businesses that are as dramatically better than what we have today as our computers and communications of today are better than the PCs of twenty years ago (Remember? 1981: 1 MHz processors, 64K of RAM, 10MB of disk and a 300 bps modem versus 2000: 800 MHz processors, 256M of RAM, 10 GB of disk, 100 Mbps LAN connection, all in a notebook computer.) Even with the limited online shopping experiences available today, the online business markets are growing with astonishing speed. How much better will it get in ten or twenty years? It will be the difference between PacMan of twenty years ago and today's elaborate worldwide virtual reality games with thousands of simultaneously interacting gamers like Ever-Quest (http://www.everquest.com). As the EverQuest site describes it:

> *Welcome to the world of EverQuest®, a real 3-D massively multi-player fantasy role-playing game. Prepare to enter an enormous virtual environment – an entire world with its own diverse species, economic systems, alliances, and politics. Choose from a variety of races and classes, and begin your quest in any number of cities or villages throughout several continents. From there, equip yourself for adventure, seek allies and knowledge, and head out into a rich world of dungeons, towers, crypts, evil abbeys – anything conceivable — even planes and realities beyond your imagination. Learn skills, earn experience, acquire treasure and equipment, meet friends and encounter enemies. A multitude of quests and adventures await, but you choose your role, you define your destiny. But whether you make yourself a noble human knight, a vicious dark elf thief, a greedy dwarven merchant, or whatever suits your desire, remember one thing: You're in our world now.*

No, it's not PacMan.

The effect on society will be profound (although it will be quickly thought of as normal, as if it has always been with us, just as every technological miracle has been regarded from electricity to air travel to antibiotics). The Net already has been significant with URLs on every bit of ad copy and mentioned as backup material on every television magazine show. (Remember, we are just five years into this thing!) Everyone will simply assume the benefits of access to enormous volumes of information and the computing power to search it, sort it, select it, distill it and apply it. Over the coming years we will see the world become not only much better informed; but each of us, through the selection power of the Net, will take control of the information we gather and the knowledge we build.

If you think the first five years of the Net have been interesting, just wait to see what comes next!

Bibliography

Allen, C., Kania, D., and Yaeckel, B. *Internet World Guide to One-To-One Web Marketing*. New York: John Wiley & Sons, 1998.

Beckwith, H. *Selling the Invisible*. New York: Warner Books, 1997.

Beckwith, H. *The Invisible Touch*. New York: Warner Books, 2000.

Berners-Lee, T. with Fischetti, M. *Weaving the Web*. New York: HarperCollins, 1999.

Bygrave, W. D. *The Portable MBA in Entrepreneurship*. New York: John Wiley & Sons, 1997.

Chase, L. with Hanger, N.C. *Internet World, Essential Business Tactics for the Net*. New York: John Wiley & Sons, 1998.

Christensen, C. M. *The Innovator's Dilemma*. Boston: Harvard Business School Press, 1997.

Collins, J. C., and Porras, J. I. *Built to Last*. New York: HarperCollins Publishers, 1997.

Creating Value in the Network Economy. Tapscott, D. (ed.). Boston: Harvard Business School Publishing, 1999.

Cusumano, M. A., and Selby R. W. *Microsoft Secrets.* New York: Touchstone, 1998.

Cusumano, M. A., and Yoffie, D. B. *Competing on Internet Time.* New York: The Free Press, 1998.

Davis, S., and Meyer, C. *Blur.* Reading, MA: Perseus Books, 1998.

Dell, M. with Fredman, C. *Direct from Dell.* New York: HarperBusiness, 1999.

Downes, L., and Mui, C. *Unleashing the Killer App.* Boston: Harvard Business School Press, 1998.

Drucker, P. F. *Innovation and Entrepreneurship.* New York: Harper & Row, 1986.

Dyson, E. *Release 2.1.* New York: Broadway Books, 1998.

Easton, J. *StrikingItRich.com.* New York: McGraw-Hill, 1999.

Evans, P., and Wurster, T. S. *Blown to Bits.* Boston: Harvard Business School Press, 2000.

Figallo, C. *Internet World, Hosting Web Communities.* New York: John Wiley & Sons, 1998.

Foster, R. N. *Innovation.* New York: Summit Books, 1986.

Future of the Electronic Marketplace, The. Leebaert, D. (ed.). Cambridge, MA: The MIT Press, 1998.

Gates, B. with Myhrvold, N. and Rinearson, P. *The Road Ahead.*

New York: Penguin Books, 1995.

Gates, B. with Hemingway, C. *Business @ the Speed of Thought*. New York: Warner Books, 1999.

Hagel, J., and Armstrong, A. G. *Net Gain*. Boston: Harvard Business School Press, 1997.

Hagel, J., and Singer, M. *Net Worth*. Boston: Harvard Business School Press, 1999.

Helmstetter, G. *Increasing Hits and Selling More on your Web Site*. New York: John Wiley & Sons, 1997.

Hughes, A. M. *Strategic Database Marketing*. Chicago: Irwin Professional Publishing, 1994.

Hunter, V. L. with Tietyen, D. *Business to Business Marketing*. Lincolnwood, IL: NTC Business Books, 1997.

Judson, B. with Kelly, K. *HyperWars*. New York: Scribner, 1999.

Kelly, K. *New Rules for the New Economy*. New York: Viking Penguin, 1998.

Modahl, M. *Now or Never*. New York: HarperCollins Publishers, 2000.

Moore, J. F. *The Death of Competition*. New York: HarperBusiness, 1997.

Mougayar, W. *Opening Digital Markets*. New York: McGraw-Hill, 1998.

Peppers, D., and Rogers, M. *Enterprise One to One*. New York: Doubleday, 1997.

Peppers, D., and Rogers, M. *The One to One Future*. New York: Doubleday, 1997.

Porter, M. E. *Competitive Advantage*. New York: The Free Press, 1985.

Porter, M. E. *Competitive Strategy*. New York: The Free Press, 1980.

Ries, A. *Focus*. New York: HarperBusiness, 1997.

Ries, A., and Ries, L. *The 22 Immutable Laws of Branding*. New York: HarperBusiness, 1998.

Ries, A., and Trout, J. *Bottom-Up Marketing*. New York: Penguin Books, 1990.

Ries, A., and Trout, J. *Positioning: The Battle for Your Mind*. New York: WarnerBooks, 1986.

Schwartz, E. I. *<Webonomics>*. New York: Broadway Books, 1997.

Schwartz, E. I. *Digital Darwinism*. New York: Broadway Books, 1999.

Sewell, C., and Brown, P. B. *Customers for Life*. New York: Doubleday, 1991.

Seybold, P. B. with Marshak, R. T. *Customers.com*. New York: Times Books, 1998.

Shapiro, C., and Varian, H. R. *Information Rules*. Boston: Harvard Business School Press, 1999.

Shaver, D. *The Next Step in Database Marketing, Consumer Guided Marketing*. New York: John Wiley & Sons, 1996.

Siegel, D. *Futurize Your Enterprise*. New York: John Wiley & Sons, 1999.

Siegel, D. *Secrets of Successful Web Sites*. Indianapolis, IN: Hayden Books, 1997.

Steele, L. W. *Managing Technology*. New York: McGraw-Hill Book Company, 1989.

Sterne, J. *What Makes People Click: Advertising on the Web*. Indianapolis, IN: Que Corporation, 1997.

Sterne, J. *World Wide Web Marketing*. New York: John Wiley & Sons, 1995.

Treacy, M., and Wiersema, F. *The Discipline of Market Leaders*. Reading, MA: Addison-Wesley Publishing Company, 1996.

Wolff, M. *Burn Rate*. New York: Simon & Schuster, 1998.

Index